Peter Loewer's
MONTH-BY-MONTH
GARDEN ALMANAC
for Indoor & Outdoor Gardening

Other Gardening Books by
Peter Loewer

The Indoor Water Gardener's How-To Handbook
Bringing the Outdoors In
Seeds and Cuttings
Growing and Decorating with Grasses
Evergreens: A Guide for Landscape, Lawn, and Garden

with Bebe Miles: *Wildflower Perennials for Your Garden*

PETER LOEWER'S
Month-by-Month
GARDEN ALMANAC
for Indoor & Outdoor Gardening

A GD/Perigee Book

Dedicated to the one true lily of the field, Jean.

Perigee Books
are published by
The Putnam Publishing Group
200 Madison Avenue
New York, New York 10016

Published simultaneously in Canada by General
Publishing Co. Limited, Toronto.
Library of Congress Cataloging in Publication Data

Loewer, H. Peter
    Peter Loewer's Month-by-month garden almanac.

    "A GD/Perigee Book."
    Bibliography: p.
    Includes index.
        1. Gardening.   2. Almanacs, American.   I. Title.
II. Title: Month-by-month garden almanac.
SB 453.L74   1983   635.9   83-8318
ISBN 0-399-50857-0

The cartoon from Webster is used with the kind permission
of Al Smith of Smith Features, Inc.

Designed by Peter Loewer
First printing, 1983
Printed in the United States of America
1   2   3   4   5   6   7   8   9   10

Contents

List of Plants Illustrated

Preface

This page is being written during the opening bars of spring. Outside my studio window the unmown fields to the south of our driveway are brown with matted grass; those to the north are still covered with six inches of snow; while the driveway itself is a series of deep holes and ruts brought about by the upheavals of the winter of 1981–82, one of the worst on record.

Yet earlier today during a short walk to our garden, I was amazed to see iris leaves still green from the previous fall; dwarf evergreens with barely a hint of damage from the cold; a row of leeks in the vegetable patch ready for harvest when the ground fully thaws; cushion pinks and creeping thyme in the rock garden with stems full and fragrant; and crocus in yellow bloom. It is still only the end of March in our Catskill Mountains home. The snow that paralyzed Chicago and buried Buffalo became a warm white blanket for gardens, making this spring one of the best in years.

Nothing in the world reflects the changes of nature better than a garden, whether "the garden" is only a shelf of African violets in a small city apartment, a plot of vegetables in the suburbs, a perennial border in the country, or a vast and grand estate. This book is a record of a year in my garden. I hope you will find the ideas helpful in making innovations in your own garden; that you will find the instructions and tips time-saving and money-saving; that you will enjoy the illustrations as well as find them useful in identifying and selecting plants for your garden; and that you will utilize the space provided to keep a handy record of your own garden this year.

Peter Loewer,
Cochecton, 1983

Introduction

The word "almanac" has a long history. It is derived either from the Byzantine-Greek word *almenikhiaka* or the Moorish-Arabic word *al-manākh,* both meaning calendar. Originally *al-manākh* meant a place where camels kneel, hence a settled spot, a peaceful area, so that the results of weather become more than a temporary disturbance to the traveler but a possible threat to home and hearth. The *al-manākh* then began to record weather and, after years of observation, gave odds as to what one might expect from the sky during the coming year.

This book bypasses the weather except for general comments on its existence. Instead, it's meant as an almanac of various items for the indoor and outdoor garden. Plants and ideas—both old and new—are suggested for each month of the year, with illustrations drawn from life and advice based on actual experience.

After the monthly entries, there is a chapter listing all the nurseries that can provide the plants, seeds, or equipment mentioned in the text. These listings are far from complete, so if you know sources not listed, kindly advise me by writing to me in care of The Putnam Publishing Group, 200 Madison Avenue, New York, N.Y. 10016.

Included, to the best of my knowledge, are the existing societies and publications dedicated to the pursuit of gardening.

The Appendix also includes metric conversion charts, one for measurement and one for temperature, plus a listing of the two recognized climate zones in the United States. An annotated bibliography is provided for further reference.

ON NAMING PLANTS

Although it's true that many plants can be recognized by their common names, many more cannot. There are, for example, seven different plants known as snakeroot: common snakeroot, black snakeroot, button snakeroot, Sampson's snakeroot, Seneca snakeroot, Virginia snakeroot, and white snakeroot.* All these names are

*The Latin names for the snakeroots are (in the same order as above): *Asarum canadense, Cimicifuga racemosa, Eryngium yuccifolium, Gentianal catesbaei, Polygala senega, Aristolochia serpentaria,* and *Eupatorium rugosum.*

now in general use. Imagine the variations on these seven across fifty states and Canada. Then imagine the confusion that would arise when one snakeroot is thought to be another in the order department of a nursery operated by someone who didn't like plants to begin with.

To prevent such confusion, all plants known to man have been given Latin or scientific names—each unique—easily understood throughout the world, whatever the language involved. In the 1700s, when the present system of classification began, Latin was the international language of scholars and seemed the obvious choice to botanists.

Four terms are in general use: *genus, species, variety,* and *cultivar.* All reference books, most gardening books, nearly all catalogs and nurseries, and even the majority of seed packets list the scientific name just under the common.

In print, the *genus* and *species* are set off from the accompanying text by the use of italics. *Genus* refers to a group of plants that are very closely related, while the *species* suggests an individual plant's quality or color or honors the person who first discovered that particular plant. Usually the *genus* is capitalized and the *species* is lower case, but when the *species* is derived from a former generic name, a person's name, or a common name, it too can begin with a capital letter.

Variety is also italicized and usually preceded by the abbreviation "var.", set in roman type. A *variety* is a plant that naturally develops by chance a noticeable change in characteristics and that breeds true from generation to generation. A *cultivar* is a variation that appears on a plant while in cultivation (thus a change either by chance or design); such a plant is called a *culti*vated *var*iety, or a cultivar, and is distinguished in type by being set in roman bold inside single quote marks.

The common garden flower known as honesty, money plant, or moonwort is grown for its seedpods that are round and silvery. The Latin name is *Lunaria annua*. One form has leaves striped with white and is called *Lunaria annua* var. *variegata,* while another cultivar with especially large purple flowers is called *Lunaria annua* **'Munstead Purple'.**

MORE NOMENCLATURE

A few other terms in general use are annual, biennial, and perennial. An annual completes the cycle of growth from seed germination to maturity, flowering, and production of new seed in one season or less than one year, then dies.

A biennial follows the same pattern but requires two growing seasons to accomplish the same.

A perennial lives many years, flowering and producing seeds every season. Within this classification are short-lived perennials that flourish for a few years, then die, and longer-lived types that last well over fifty years in one garden.

IMPORTING PLANTS FROM OVERSEAS

One of the best sources for unusual plants is England. Although it's becoming harder to import plants, the dedicated gardener continues to do so and often sends past Europe to China and the Far East.

The United States is ever vigilant in guarding against imported pests and diseases (remember the Japanese beetle and the gypsy moth?), and all plants imported from foreign countries are closely watched for dangerous immigrants. If you wish to import plants, you must have an Import Permit for Plants and Plant Products that assigns you a registration number and permit stamps that *you* must send to the seller along with each order. These stamps advise the seller that unless the plants are washed clean of soil and packed in a sterile medium like sphagnum moss, they will not be allowed into the United States. Although, as with any government activity, it takes time to get a permit, the service is free. Just write to:

United States Department of Agriculture
Animal and Plant Health Inspection Service
Plant Protection and Quarantine Programs
Federal Center Building
Hyattsville, Maryland 20782

The forms make the procedure look a bit complicated, but it really isn't, and most nurseries throughout the world are quite familiar with the procedure. Remember to allow time for the shipments, and try to place orders by early spring in the Northeast.

These restrictions do not apply to buying seeds through the mail.

The ALMANAC •

Announced by all the trumpets of the sky,
Arrives the snow, and, driving o'er the fields,
Seems nowhere to alight: the withered air
Hides hills and woods, the river, and the heaven,
And veils the farm-house at the garden's end.
The sled and traveller stopped, the courier's feet
Delayed, all friends shut out, the housemates sit
Around the radiant fireplace, enclosed
In a tumultuous privacy of storm.
    RALPH WALDO EMERSON, *The Snow-Storm*

Often when we are lost in that limbo between the days of Christmas and the wakening spirit of Easter, when skies can be overly dark with barren branches whipped by chilling winds, we easily forget the reasons behind the changing of the seasons. But think a moment about a garden forever warm, forever growing, always green, with brilliant dots of color every day of the year—a garden that never rests. There would be no time to plan, no moments to quietly sit and reflect on the triumphs and failures of the preceding seasons, no chance for change.

And the muted colors of winter would be gone. We would miss the only time of the year when the landscape becomes a sheet of paper and all upon it the dark lines of pen, only here and there a watercolor touch of faded brown or that particular orange of a winter's setting sun when it lights the final twilight glow along the horizon.

THE CYCLAMEN

The first rays of dawn were reflected through long icicles that clung to the greenhouse eaves, results of a January thaw on the previous day. The cold light glistened on some thirty blossoms that hovered on long stems over a pot of florist's cyclamen *(Cyclamen persicum giganteum)* that I've kept going for over twelve years.

Of all the flowering gift plants of the Christmas season, this is my favorite, but if unable to find a cool place for this plant, never buy one. If yours is a gift, enjoy the flowers while you can, then give it away to a friend who lives in colder surroundings. Since the original plants came from the mountains of Persia where the climate is cool and bright, warm rooms of above 60°F. shorten flower life and prevent immature buds from ever opening. You can try moving the

THE GARDEN IN WINTER

A garden in winter need not be as dismal as it sounds. The backyard pictured at left is stocked with plants, shrubs, and small trees that keep their visual interest throughout the year. (1) The teasel (*Dipsacus sylvestris*) leaves prickly seed-heads after flowering in the second year of growth; once established, this biennial reseeds for yearly flowers. (2) Dried seedheads of gloriosa daisies (*Rudbeckia hirta* cultivars) or perennial coneflowers. (3) An old-fashioned rambling rose with red rose hips. (4) A red-stemmed dogwood (*Cornus alba* 'Sibirica'). (5) The six-to-eight-foot canes of eulalia grass (*Miscanthus sacchariflorus*). (6) A hybrid rhododendron. (7) Harry Lauder's walking stick (*Corylus avellana* 'Contorta'). (8) A dwarf Alberta spruce (*Picea glauca* 'Conica'). (9) A weeping birch (*Betula pendula* 'Tristis'). (10) The seedheads of a garden sedum (*Sedum Telephium*). (11) Maiden grass, a smaller relative of eulalia (*Miscanthus sinensis* 'Gracillimus'). (12) A gray birch (*Betula populifolia*). The tree on the hillside silhouetted against a winter sky is an old and gnarled apple tree left for its visual interest.

1

CYCLAMENS

On the previous page are four cyclamens that make excellent houseplants if given a cool environment (not above 60°F. in wintertime), plenty of moisture and humidity, and a good rest during the heat of summer. Clockwise from top left *Cyclamen hederifolium* with its beautifully patterned foliage of light and dark greens touched with maroon; *C. repandum,* a smaller plant that produces pinwheel flowers of intense pink; *C. persicum,* with dark green leaves and perfumed flowers of pink to white; and the flowers of florist's cyclamen *(C. persicum giganteum),* the gift plant of Christmas.

Lemongrass

plant closer to a window, where temperatures are always cooler, but the plant will eventually wear itself out from heat.

Most garden books tell a cyclamen owner to dry the tuber—the corky-brown "bulb" that sits like a rounded potato on the soil's surface — after winter flowering is over, allowing it to dry out completely for the summer. The year I tried that approach, the field mice entered the greenhouse and cheerfully consumed the tubers.

Then I found cultural instructions in an old English garden book, circa 1890, that advised keeping the plant in growth all year long. Eventually the leaves will yellow and die, but they soon will be replaced by a new crop. I tried this approach and the plant described above is one result.

The florist's cyclamen is available in hybrids of many striking shades of red, with either single or double blossoms; a pure white to a white just touched with pink; salmon; coral; and deep, deep maroon.

Use a standard houseplant soil with an addition of one-third sand by volume and a pot at least one inch wider than the width of the tuber. Late spring and summer are the best times to repot.

The soil should never be allowed to completely dry out or the whole plant will wilt, leaves and flowers quickly drooping over the edge of the pot. If this happens to you, don't despair. Take newspaper and completely surround the pot, starting at one side and slowly pulling the stems into an upright position, much like a florist wrapping a bouquet. Fasten the paper with tape or staples and immediately soak the soil. Before the day is out, the stems should absorb enough water to hold themselves up. Never wait too long to institute this procedure or the plant will die back and be forced to produce new leaves, and will not have enough strength for more flowers until next season. A self-watering pot or water wicks (you will need more than one wick for a large plant) are a big help.

Water should never be poured directly on or into the slight depression on the top of the tuber as it could produce a case of rotting. This doesn't mean that an occasional few drops will destroy the plant, but it's a good habit to take care in watering.

Give plants sun in summer, except during the heat of midday. Set them out-of-doors in a place where some shade will be provided. Fertilize established plants every two weeks in summer and once a month during winter.

When removing dead flowers or leaves, give the stems a sharp twist before pulling them away from the tubers.

Plants are easily grown from seed and will produce flowers in eighteen months from germination.

For growing cyclamens outside in colder climates, see notes for September.

LEMONGRASS

Southern Florida, parts of California, and Hawaii are the only states where it is warm enough to grow lemongrass *(Cymbopogon citratus)* out-of-doors. But it does very well as a houseplant in the rest of the country and becomes a beautiful specimen plant if left outside for the summer, always giving it as much sun as possible.

The grass rarely tops four feet in a pot but can go well over six feet in the tropics. The leaves are the commercial source of lemon oil and it's always a great conversation piece when you ask visitors to crush a bit of leaf between their fingers and the bright, fresh smell of lemons is the result.

Use a standard potting soil, and when the roots begin to peek through the pot's drainage hole, pot on to one size larger. Soil should be lightened with sand for good drainage (one-third sand, two-thirds soil), and fertilizer monthly whenever growth is evident.

There is another use for this grass: It's one of the main food flavorings in all cooking from Thailand. There the plant is called *takrai* and is either grown in the Thai home or purchased at the neighborhood market, both fresh and dried. You might find the dried form in the spice departments of the larger supermarkets in America.

The following recipe, while somewhat hot to American taste, is absolutely delicious. In addition to the lemongrass, you will need fish sauce or Nam Pla, available in most of the larger gourmet shops.

Shrimp Soup with Lemongrass (4 to 6 servings)

1½ quarts of chicken broth
1 tablespoon dried lemongrass
⅛ teaspoon hot pepper seeds (or to taste)
Juice of one large lemon
Dash of Nam Pla
½ pound raw, small, shelled, shrimps, deveined
3 to 4 chopped green onions
5 to 6 sprigs of fresh or dried coriander

Bring the broth to a boil in a saucepan and drop in the lemongrass, torn into small pieces. Continue to boil for five minutes and add pepper seeds, lemon juice, and fish sauce. Lower heat and add the shrimp. Cook three to four minutes until the shrimps are opaque and pink. Add green onions and coriander. Serve at once.

THE JANUARY THAW

It is difficult to believe that winter has weeks to go when the January thaw presents itself. That warm sun in a clear blue sky can lull you with a false sense of security, especially when the snow level starts to fall: mouse prints enlarge—dog prints loom as bear's — as their imprinted edges pull away with the melt; snow fleas (*Achorutes nivicolus*) bounce across the sparkling surface, and one peculiar variety of crane fly (*Trichocera* spp.) suddenly appears outside the kitchen window, bobbing up and down in the warming air.

The action of warm days and cold nights first melts the snow then freezes again and many plants with shallow or immature root systems (not to mention all those plastic labels) rise out of the

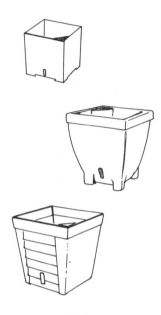

SELF-WATERING POTS

All self-watering pots follow the same principle: A plastic or Styrofoam grid or platform holds the soil as water is drawn up by a nylon or fiber glass wick from a reservoir below. The soil grid is held above water level by a hollow tube or by supports that spring from the inside surface of the pot. If the reservoir is full, you can usually avoid watering for up to three weeks depending on the pot's size. By adding fertilizer to the water and using a soilless mix of vermiculite and peat moss, many plants do well as hydroponic subjects.

Water wicks are the size of heavy wrapping twine some six inches or more in length. One end is placed in a container of water and the other inserted in the pot's soil. They work by capillary action and can be made by braiding tufts of fiber glass—but wear gloves when doing this as fiber glass is irritating to even normal skin.

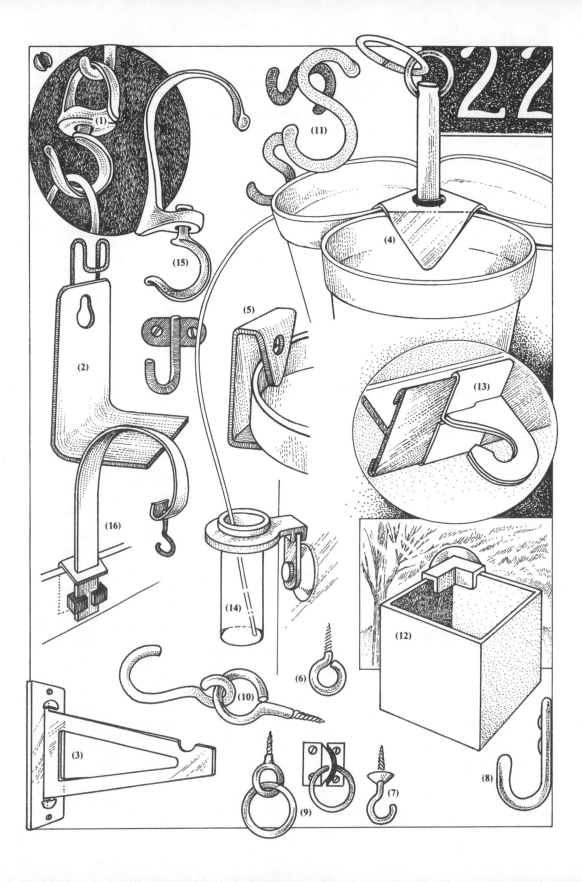

ground. It is up to the gardener to push them gently back so they will not die of exposure in early spring.

Another good idea is to mulch your flower beds with pine branches left from your Christmas tree or a light covering of hay. The idea here is to keep the ground under the mulch pjotected from the sun so the ground stays frozen and the act of heaving is prevented. Contrary to popular belief, mulching is not meant to keep plants warm. If the winter snows come early, do not melt in a thaw, and stay upon the ground until spring, the follow. g garden year is usually superb.

By now the seed catalogs should be arriving in earnest. Each Technicolor production of print and paper is bound (excuse the pun) to please the gardener with visions of what is to come. But hold off —don't succumb quite yet; wait until they all arrive and order your seeds when the days are a bit longer, when the weight of winter is not quite as heavy as now.

Start with plans for seed germination: Save orange-juice containers, coffee cans, milk and cream cartons, even egg cartons, for future plants.

HANG-UPS

For years the only solution to hanging up a plant was the cup hook working in conjunction with a bent coat hanger, no matter what the result did to a room's decor. Then came the green revolution of the seventies and plants turned up everywhere, covering all available tables and shelves, niches and corners. Designers were forced to look up at the ceiling, and the result is the drawing at left showing seventeen different items of hardware capable of holding up your houseplants with a minimum of effort.

(1) The swivel hook makes it easy to rotate your hanging plants. (2) A metal hanger will support large pots. (3) The swivel plant bracket is made of clear plastic, holds plants up to twelve inches in diameter, and swings in a 180° arc. (4) The tri-pot holder is a plant chandelier from England that holds three flowerpots (three, four, or five inches in diameter) on a thirteen-inch chain. (5) This flowerpot holder is a plated metal clip that will hold flowerpots on a wall. (6) A screw eye from the hardware store. (7) Cup hook. (8) Clothes hooks. (9) Both forms are hitching rings. (10) Hammock hooks are four inches long and when screwed into a solid beam of wood will hold a great deal of weight. (11) S hooks look better than bent wires and hold up to thirty pounds. (12) Window planter with super-mold suction bracket attaches a white plastic container to mirrors, windows, or sliding glass doors. (13) Barnacle is a display hook designed to work in pairs and meant for suspended ceilings, holding reasonable weight if the ceiling grid itself is strong. (14) Root 1® easily adheres to windows, mirrors, or any smooth surface with a clear plastic suction cup; it will work with water as a rooter or dry as a fanciful floral container. (15) Big Hook Swivel is large enough to hang planters on curtain rods, pipes, branches — just about any overhead rod or ledge—and is able to hold up to thirty pounds. (16)

HANG-UPS
   The drawing at the left shows many of the hardware items available today for holding up houseplants with a minimum of effort.

E-Z Mount ®Screwless Plant Hanger mounts on window trim without screws and comes with a swivel hook that loops out over drapes and curtain rods and can be installed without tools or making holes in the woodwork.

READING THE WEATHER

Rather than depend on the often incorrect weather forecasts of television, why not make your own wind vane on a cold winter's evening, purchase an inexpensive barometer, and, using the accompanying chart, become your own weather forecaster? In so doing, you will be able to know on the spot whether the weather will be cooperating in the garden.

WIND-BAROMETER TABLE

Wind Direction	Barometer (Reduced to Sea Level)	Character of Weather Indicated
E to N	29.80 or below— barometer falling rapidly	Severe northeast gale and heavy rain. In winter, heavy snow, followed by cold wave.
E to NE	30.10 and above— falling slowly	Summer, with light winds: Rain may not fall for several days. Winter: rain within 24 hours.
E to NE	30.10 and above— falling rapidly	Summer: Rain probable within 12 to 24 hours. Winter R or S, increasing winds.
SE to NE	30.10 to 30.20— falling slowly	Rain in 12 to 18 hours.
SE to NE	30.10 to 30.20— falling rapidly	Increasing wind, with rain within 12 hours.
SE to NE	30.00 or below— falling slowly	Rain will continue 1 to 2 days.
SE to NE	30.00 or below— falling rapidly	Rain with high wind, followed within 36 hours by clearing, and in winter, by colder weather.
S to E	29.80 or below— falling rapidly	Severe storm imminent, followed within 24 hours by clearing, and in winter by colder weather.
S to SE	30.10 to 30.20— falling slowly	Rain within 24 hours.
S to SE	30.10 to 30.20— falling rapidly	Increasing wind, with rain within 12 to 24 hours.
Going to W	29.80 or below— rising rapidly	Clearing and colder.
S to SW	30.00 or below— rising slowly	Clearing within a few hours, then fair for several days.
SW to NW	30.10 to 30.20— barometer steady	Fair with slight temperature changes for 1 to 2 days.
SW to NW	30.10 to 30.20— rising rapidly	Fair, followed within 2 days by rain.

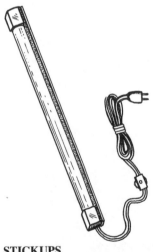

STICKUPS

A new fluorescent plant light called Gro & Sho® is being marketed by General Electric. It installs in minutes and comes complete with cord and switch. The lamp is twenty-five inches long and ready to brighten most any corner.

SW to NW	30.20 and above— barometer steady	Continued fair, with no definite temperature change.
SW to NW	30.20 and above— falling slowly	Fair for 2 days, with slowly rising temperature.

Wind-Chill Factor

Temperature					Wind Speed				
	Calm	5	10	15	20	25	30	35	40
+50	50	48	40	36	32	30	28	27	26
+40	40	37	28	22	18	16	13	11	10
+30	30	27	16	9	4	0	−2	−4	−6
+20	20	16	4	−5	−10	−15	−18	−20	−21
+10	10	6	−9	−18	−25	−29	−33	−35	−37
0	0	−5	−21	−36	−39	−44	−48	−50	−53
−10	−10	−15	−33	−45	−53	−59	−63	−67	−69
−20	−20	−26	−46	−58	−67	−74	−79	−82	−85
−30	−30	−36	−58	−72	−82	−88	−94	−98	−100
−40	−40	−47	−70	−88	−96	−104	−109	−113	−116

Calm: Chimney smoke rises vertically.
1–12 mph: Leaves stir; you feel a breeze on your face.
13–24 mph: Branches stir; loose paper is blown about.
25–30 mph: Large branches move; wires whistle.
30–40 mph: Whole trees in motion; hard to walk against the wind.

THE WIND-CHILL FACTOR

When planting many perennials, the gardener must remember the effect that wind has on temperature, and what better time to note the chill than the depth of winter. A calm 0° F. is really not so bad at all, but when combined with a 20-mph wind, it becomes an unbearable −39° F. And the same discomfort is felt by many garden plants and trees. By carefully selecting protected spots for questionably hardy plants, you can cut your losses for the next winter.

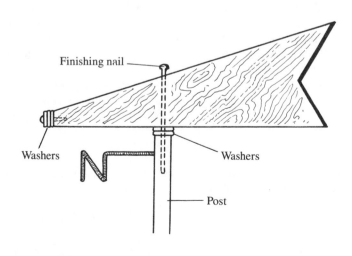

Finishing nail

Washers

Washers

Post

A WIND VANE

Cut a piece of ¼-inch plywood (marine grade) in the shape of an arrow, with the vane end having more surface than the front. Finding the center of balance, drill a hole through the vane and mount it on a headless (or finishing) nail that has been hammered into a post. Use a few washers or a wooden bead as indicated in the drawing. Find north with a compass and make indicators of N, S, E, and W out of bent wire. Add a few small washers to the front end with a small screw for additional weight.

DORMANCY

Everything in life must rest at one time or another, and plants are no exception to the rule. After they have finished with flowering and leaves have been able to manufacture sufficient food for the next year, plants will usually enter a period of dormancy. This quiet time in a plant's life is governed by a natural cycle of growth: a combination of day length, temperature fluctuation, and the availability of water.

The process is especially noticeable in the temperate regions of the world where leaves turn color and fall; even bonsai subjects will exhibit this change. But tropical plants are not so obvious as they hold most of their leaves throughout the year. Neither kind will continue to be fruitful, flower, or bear new leaves on a year-round basis. If they are forced to overwork for long periods of time, they will ultimately die, literally worn out from overwork.

Plants brought in from out-of-doors will slow their growth for winter; wildflowers and spring blubs will not produce flowers at all if not given a rest at an average temperature of 40°F.

In the northern hemisphere, when plants give signs of halting their growth as days shorten and temperatures fall, do not despair— with advancing spring they will awaken. Until such time, watering should be kept to a minimum, just enough to keep stems and leaves from shriveling. Fertilizing should be stopped entirely.

STRAWBERRIES FROM SEED

A new development on the horticultural horizon is the 'Sweetheart' strawberry to be introduced to the public for the 1983 garden season. The surprise is that 'Sweetheart' is grown from seeds, not cuttings; will bear 140 days after sowing; and 70 percent of the plants will flower and fruit the first year.

By starting plants from seed in January or February, they can go out to the garden after danger of frost and either be treated as annuals or given winter protection for bearing the second year.

Seeds should be germinated at 60°–65°F., transplanted, and grown on as other garden plants. Up north, plant seeds indoors during week 1, transplant into individual containers in week 6, move outside at week 12, with first flowers forming in week 18, and berry production until the first frost of autumn. In southern climes, sow the seeds indoors from July through September, then follow the same weekly schedule.

One of the beauties of this new plant is its adaptability to either the open ground or hanging pots and containers. Remember to water well.

HINTS FOR JANUARY

When watering your houseplants, be sure that the water is at room temperature—or above if you are saving fuel!

Make a rough plan of your annual—or cutting—garden.

AN OLD BEGONIA

The begonia pictured on the opposite page is an old-fashioned "beefsteak begonia" *(Begonia × erythrophylla)* taken from a cutting provided by my sister-in-law's plant of some ten years. Hers, in turn, was taken from a specimen plant at least fifty years old belonging to her great-aunt Tess, and the years roll by. At one time everybody had one of these begonias, but fashions change and more exotic types appeared on the horizon. But don't be fooled: For a houseplant companion to go on year after year with a minimum of care but bloom in profusion every January and February is something of a rarity. If you have a shady spot with morning or afternoon sun, where temperatures fluctuate between 50° and 65°F., this is your plant. Keep the soil evenly moist. (For more on begonia care, see the entry for October.)

**THE GYPSY MOTH
IN WINTER**

Now that the leaves are gone and winter has hit with a vengeance, what better time to take a walk about your property and look for the egg masses left by the previous season's gypsy moths before they so justly perished.

The eggs will usually be at eye level, sometimes slightly below, and on occasion ten to twelve feet up a trunk. They will be massed in oval puffs of light-tan felt, each puff some two inches long, and there they will sit by the thousands, secure between ridges of bark, waiting for the warmth of spring to hatch into marauding armies of bristly caterpillars.

Using a twig or stick, scrape the eggs into a bag and burn them. Merely breaking up the felty mass and dashing it on the ground with an oath is a useless display of energy; the individual eggs will merely hatch by themselves close to the spot where you threw them, after the melting snows bring them closer to the warming earth.

Obviously this is but one small step in a continuing march—but a step well worth taking.

Check your evergreens for snow damage.

If you live in the country, check pots of bulbs for mouse damage, for dig they must!

Nothing does a better job on field mice in the garden—or rabbits, for that matter—than a large and hungry cat.

This is a good time to order garden supplies.

On a good January day — if any — take a walk and check your ornamental trees for egg cases of gypsy moths. Scrape the eggs into a coffee can and burn, burn, burn!

Make sure that your amaryllises are not forgotten now that they may have flowered.

Check any stored bulbs, corms, or tubers for decay. Destroy them if too far gone.

Wood ashes from the Franklin or wood stove are fine for the garden.

Check your cactus collection. Do they need any water?

As the snow piles up, make sure your fences are adequate for protection from animals; small rabbits need only small spaces....

NOTES

FEBRUARY

In every year there are days between winter and spring which rightly belong to neither; days when the round of seasons seems to be at a standstill, as though the inner impulse which held on visibly enough through the worst of the hard weather had failed just when it should begin to quicken towards the first of the better times....

There are evenings...when the world is as nearly unlovely as it ever can be under natural conditions: the air cold with a sodden chill that bites worse than frost; land and sky wrapped in a dim cloud without form or motion; the year altogether at its worst, foul from the winter, frostbitten, flood-swept, sunk in a sapless lethargy when it is more than time for the stirrings of the yearly miracle of repair.

ANONYMOUS, from *Corners of Old Grey Gardens*

February can be bleak, it's true, but the month always seems mercifully short, a combination of the ever-lasting days and the foresight of the calendar planners who decided that this was the month to take out a nip of time.

From the gardener's point of view, there is much to be done: Flowering bulbs scent the air, orders for next season's seed and plants must be completed, and it's time to finally sit down and put together an electric seedbed.

THE AMARYLLIS

Surely the queen of the winter window is the amaryllis (pictured at left), a family of flowering bulbs with more than seventy members that hail from tropical America (with one member from Africa), belonging to the genus *Hippeastrum*.

The bulbs can be left out-of-doors in the southern tip of Florida, a bit of southern Texas (where it touches Mexico and the Gulf), and a few small areas of California. Elsewhere this is a potted houseplant with a sojourn to the backyard during the heat of summer. *Amaryllis* is the old genus name, no longer used; *Hippeus* means knight on horseback, and *astron*, a star. The star is easy to figure, the knight is not.

If your first bulb is a gift, fully packaged and/or potted when you receive it, follow the directions on the package and repot it in the autumn that follows blooming, when the leaves turn yellow and die back.

In spring, plant a barren bulb in a soil mix of one-third potting soil, one-third sand, and one-third composted cow manure, placing the bulb halfway into a pot no more than two inches larger in diameter than the bulb. Firm the soil but leave the top part of the

AMARYLLIS FROM SEED

Cross-pollinating your own amaryllis hybrids is a fascinating hobby. Try to pick two parents of pure color—red with red, or orange with orange—and, using a small watercolor brush, take pollen from the anthers of one flower and brush it on the stigma of the second. Separate the parent plant from the others and remove its anthers so it sheds no pollen.

When the pods ripen and burst, black seeds will appear, stacked like slices of bread. Sow seeds in sphagnum moss or a prepared growing mix, covering them lightly. Using a growing temperature of 60°–65° F., seeds should germinate within ten to fifteen days. When seedlings are large enough to handle, place ten in a six-inch pot and keep them at the same temperature as during germination.

When the leaves are six inches long, pot each plant individually in a four-inch pot using the recommended mix. Until they flower for the first time, never let them dry out.

Be sure to keep accurate records of your trials and errors.

AN EXPERIMENT

Last year I had an extra amaryllis bulb and, instead of potting it in soil, I placed the bulb over water, using a jam jar and a circular support cut from a piece of heavy acetate. Soon the leaves began to grow and the bulb produced long white roots, the tips covered with tiny hairs. In six weeks the bulb produced a stalk and bloomed with three flowers.

I've kept it in water, changing the water every three weeks and adding a weak solution of liquid plant food once every month. As of now (February 1983), the bulb has been going for thirteen months.

The room it's in is cool, usually 55°F. I will now move it to warmer quarters. Perhaps it will bloom....

BULBS IN WATER

The drawing on the previous pages shows the following plants growing in water (from left): a Roman hyacinth *(Hyacinthus orientalis)*, crocus *(Crocus vernus)*, an avocado pit *(Persea americana)*, devil's-tongue *(Sauromatum guttatum)*, Soleil d'Or narcissus *(Narcissus tazetta)*, the amaryllis, and another small crocus.

The devil's-tongue should be allowed to dry out in October and kept dry for the winter at a temperature of not less than 50°F.

The avocado must eventually be potted in soil.

The other bulbs are generally thrown away after blooming.

bulb (about one-quarter) uncovered. Keep the soil moist but not wet. After the leaves appear, feed the plant liquid plant food every month during growth. Give the bulb at least four hours or more of full sun with about 50°F. at night and 70°F. or more during the day. Every summer after the first year, replace the top inch of soil with fresh, and pot on every three years. In time a healthy bulb can produce many flowers and attain a circumference of some fourteen inches.

From late October to mid-December, keep the bulb slightly drier and allow a rest. When you wish to start bloom, bring the pot into an area of about 70°F. and place it in a dim or dark spot. When the flower stalk is some six inches high, place the plant in a sunny window.

Remove the flowers after blossoming is completed unless you wish to set seed. Seedlings will bloom in three to four years after germination.

GROWING BULBS IN WATER

Up to a few years ago, the idea of planting bulbs in water was considered old hat, something of little value that the fusty Victorians enjoyed. But nothing can be quite as lovely and encouraging to the spirit as the sight of spring flowers glowing in a water-filled container on a window sill or coffee table.

Forcing spring bulbs is not very expensive, requires no fantastic equipment—although you could spend a fortune collecting truly antique hyacinth glasses from Victorian times—and very easy to accomplish. While a rich garden soil might eventually produce a showier flower, it's not needed—the flower is already formed, small and perfect, covered by the leaf layers of the bulb. What you are doing is speeding up the timetable of the seasons, convincing the bulbs that January and February are really March and April.

Two types of flowering bulbs are available: the hardy outdoor types like hyacinth, crocus, and lily-of-the-valley (technically not a bulb but a rootstock called a "pip") and the more tender bulbs that will not withstand a northern winter—for example, paper-whites, Soleil d'Or, and Chinese sacred lilies, all varieties of *Narcissi tazetta.*

These bulbs can all be purchased from garden catalogs or garden-supply stores during the autumn months. Part of the preparations for winter blooming have already been done for you by the nurseries: The bulbs have been preconditioned to bloom early by controlled fluctuations in temperature. Caution: Never let any of these bulbs dry out once you have started the cycle of growth, for they will not survive such treatment.

Fill containers with water so that the bottoms of the bulbs give the wet just a glancing touch, then place the containers in a cool place (40°–50°F.) and total darkness. Check to see that the water level is kept up and wait for the white roots to form; this usually takes about a month.

When the white, twining roots have filled the glass container, remove them to a cool, shady area for about five days. Then you can place them in a sunny window (preferrably in a cool room), rotating the container daily so the flower stalks remain reasonably straight as they grow.

If your hyacinth should start to bloom before the buds are away from the bulb, cover with an inverted paper cone until the stem is long enough.

ORDERING SEEDS

If you are a member of any of the plant societies (Royal Horticultural Society, American Rock Garden Society, Alpine Garden Society, Scottish Rock Garden Society, American Primrose Society) or have sent to the many seed companies for catalogs, now is the time to make sure that you have made your choices and sent out your orders.[*]

Membership dues vary, and catalog costs are usually very low. And there is not a better way to expand your garden (and houseplant) collections since many of these groups list some specimens only found in the far corners of the world and collected by museum or society expeditions on special assignment.

A RADIANT HEATER

The Sun-gro Radiant Heater is just the thing for warming the feet of your tropical plants (either in water or dirt) when the chills of winter become too much for their tender constitutions. The surface temperature is held to approximately 120°F. with a thermostat that cuts it off when it reaches that level. When used in growing plants that unit should be kept at least three-inches away and don't place seed flats directly on the surface without using an insulating layer. The only problem is care with water spillage, as with any electrical appliance.

Cost is low, drawing a maximum of 60 watts, or about an average of $2.50 a month for continuous operation.

According to the manufacturer, in an open room with a 68°F. temperature maintained, one unit with two growing lamps will sprout tomato seeds in flats placed in shallow water pans within seven days.

Besides if your plants are warm enough, it's truly great for cold and human feet.

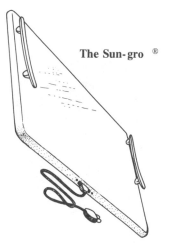

The Sun-gro ®

FLOWERS IN FEBRUARY

Two years ago I bought a packet of wallflower seeds of mixed colors *(Cheiranthus cheiri)* from a Page Seed Company display at the local general store. Below a beautiful color shot of many blooms, the label identified it as a biennial but not hardy in our zone 5. I planted the seeds in early February, hoping to have flowers by September.

---

[*] See appendix 4 for a complete list of seed sources.

Wallflowers

Prayer plant

I had first seen the vibrant colors of these flowers and smelled their rich fragrance when walking in England's Kew Gardens. In fact most of London in April and May is bedecked with window boxes bursting with these blooms.

Mine did not bloom the first year, but the plants were about two feet tall with heavy, woody stems forming at the base, so I put them in the cool greenhouse for the winter where temperatures would stay between 35° and 45°F. By January the plants had lost a few leaves but looked green and healthy.

Then, around the first of February, I noticed that buds were forming in the hollow between the newest leaves at the tips of the three-foot branches. Each day they grew, to open on February 22 with flowers of the deepest velvet purple and a perfume that reached to every corner of the greenhouse. The plants continued to bloom with orange, yellow, white, white-and-orange, and more purples for another two months as I removed the dead flowers before they set seed.

In their native haunts of southern Europe, these plants grow in stone walls and sandy soil, so use a soil mix of at least one-half sand.

Although plants are perennial, they are best treated as biennials, for the older plants become sparse and rangy with little bloom.

THE PRAYER PLANT

The red-winged prayer plant *(Maranta leuconeura erythroneura)* is a member of a tropical family that fold their leaves at night. Three species are widely grown as houseplants, but the red-veined is perhaps the most beautiful; its five-inch-long leaves show a herringbone design of carmine red laid over a velvety olive green that turns a lighter shade at leaf edge, topped off with a center width of silver green. When happy in a warm and humid atmosphere with evenly moist soil and a rest in January and February, they produce small lilac flowers on eight-inch stems in early spring.

You must watch out for spider mites whenever humidity is low. These pests favor this particular plant. It's a good idea to mist the leaves and the surrounding air every day.

Use a standard potting mix and fertilize once a month when plants are in active growth.

AN ELECTRIC SEED FLAT

Right about now in a northern winter, the ice and snow are building up on the roof and, if you live in an older home, starting their inexorable spread throughout the gutter system (much like saturated fats in the body), intensifying your desire for spring. And what better way to satisfy the urge for springtime activity than to prepare a good and sturdy seedbed that maintains a constant temperature to ensure seed germination.

Most of the troubles with germinating seeds are due to the fact that the seedbeds become too cold and seeds rot in the moisture before they become warm enough to sprout. The best solution is to use a waterproof, insulated heating cable. They are sold with or without thermostats. I suggest that you invest the little bit more for the thermostat model (usually preset to 70°F.) just to be on the safe side and prevent overheating. Cables vary in length from 12 to 120 feet.

The accompanying drawing shows a simply constructed seedbed made from easily obtained materials. Just adjust the dimensions to the cable size you prefer.

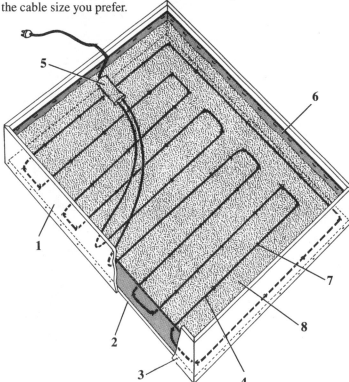

(1) ¾" x 4" planking. (2) ½" x ¾" waterproof plywood. (3) Aluminum nails. (4) Heating cable. (5) Thermostat. (6) Heavy plastic sheeting over the plywood. (7) Staples. (8) Sand and/or gravel filler that covers the cable and helps to evenly distribute the heat.

The cable is held in place with staples—just be careful not to pierce the insulation. Leave about three inches between the adjacent rows. Keep the cable away from the thermostat, as it would shut off the current before the sand or soil is properly heated, and do not overlap or cross pieces of cable.

I generally sow seeds in small peat pots, using sphagnum moss as a germinating medium, placing a dozen or so of the pots in a plastic tray, then putting the whole affair on the seedbed surface.

FORSYTHIA IN THE SPRING

Now that days are getting longer and spring is on the way, branches of forsythia can be cut and brought indoors for blooming after about ten days' exposure to the warmth of a heated room.

When temperatures are well above freezing, cut branches into two- to three-foot sections and place in lukewarm water. Remember not to take too many or there might be nothing left for outdoor bloom — although that seems doubtful when one remembers the wealth of yellow that this bush produces in early spring.

The flowers are already formed the previous fall and merely await heat and water to open in your living room.

If you are lucky enough to live near a wetlands, gather some pussy willows for indoor decoration. Keep the branches in water where they normally send out roots and you may then plant them in a moist area on your property.

Other miscellaneous branches gathered from trees and shrubs will open into leaf under indoor conditions and become a welcome preview of the seasons to come.

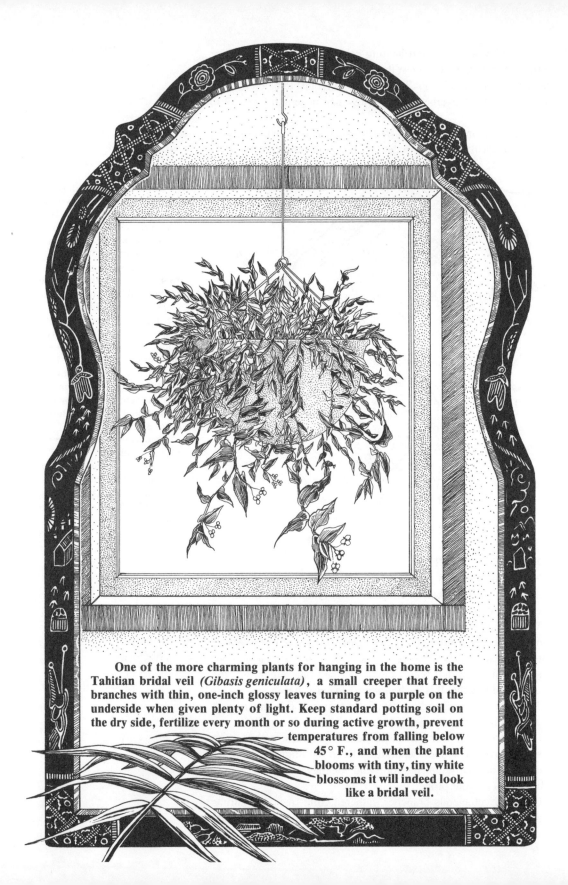

One of the more charming plants for hanging in the home is the Tahitian bridal veil *(Gibasis geniculata)*, a small creeper that freely branches with thin, one-inch glossy leaves turning to a purple on the underside when given plenty of light. Keep standard potting soil on the dry side, fertilize every month or so during active growth, prevent temperatures from falling below 45° F., and when the plant blooms with tiny, tiny white blossoms it will indeed look like a bridal veil.

SEED-GROWING MEDIUMS

Most of the major seed companies now offer seed-starter kits that are almost foolproof, and each year sees more products hit the market.

As a seed-growing medium, sphagnum moss is my first choice. It's tidy and free of contaminating organisms, whereas nonsterile mediums tend to favor the development of a fungus that causes a disease called "damping-off," which destroys seedlings as they emerge from the soil.

Sphagnum moss

The term "sphagnum" identifies several different mosses found in local swamps and bogs. The moss grows slowly, the lower parts gradually packing together under the weight of the plants nearer the surface and eventually forming a compact mass that is sold as peat.

Sphagnum leaves are long and hollow with a fantastic ability to absorb water. Coupled with a natural sterility (caused by a slight antiseptic quality in the plant cells), they make an exceptional medium for seed germination. Indeed, during World War I, sphagnum mosses were used as battlefield dressings because of this sterile quality.

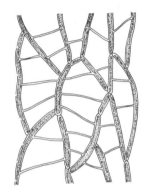

Large, open cells

Like all peats, they are intially difficult to get wet, so I suggest you mix the dried moss with water in a plastic bag, using four cups of sphagnum to one and one-half cups of warm water. The moss then must be kept continually moist or it will form a hard surface crust that will actually repel water.

Sphagnum is sold both milled and unmilled. Either one will work for germination, but the milled is easier to handle.

Put the moistened medium in flats, old coffee cans, or even halved milk cartons, patting it down especially in corners and around the edges until the surface is level.

Because there are absolutely no nutrients in sphagnum, fertilizers must be added when the true leaves appear on your seedlings.

If you are worried as to how deeply seeds must be planted, use the following guide: Seeds one-sixteenth of an inch or larger should be covered by the thickness of one seed; tinier seeds need not be covered at all, but just settled in with a light spray of water from a hand mister. A few seeds actually need light to germinate, so be sure to check cultural instructions on the package.

When sowing smaller seeds, try placing them in a piece of folded paper and tapping them out gently as you move it across the surface of the sphagnum.

Containers

CORIANDER

Coriander *(Coriandrum sativum)* is a double-use herb: The ripe seeds impart a delicate flavor of light lemon touched with anise when dried and crushed; while the fernlike, lacy leaves (known as cilentro or Chinese celery) deal a strong, pungent taste—coupled with a stronger smell—that is relished everywhere in the world except America.

This herb is one of the first used in the history of cooking and agriculture. It's been found in Egyptian tombs, is mentioned in the

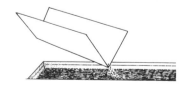

Coriander

Bible, and was first dubbed "coriander" by the Greeks from their word *koris,* meaning bug, as they assumed that the strong odor would repel insects (which it does not seem to do with any fervor).

Coriander is an annual growing to one to two feet in height. Plant seed in at least a four-inch pot using a standard mix of any good potting soil cut one-third with sand for drainage. Cover the seed with one-quarter inch of soil, provide bottom heat, and germination should begin within fourteen days.

It's doubtful that your plants will bloom indoors unless provided with at least six hours of sunlight or the equivalent in artificial light, but the leaves will introduce you to a new flavor in cooking. Sow new seeds every three weeks to guarantee a continuous supply, and as spring looms on the horizon, keep a few plants for the outdoor herb garden, where they will flower and provide seed for the next winter.

Leaves are called *yuen sai* in Chinese and should be picked for seasoning when about six inches high. Use as a garnish on Indian curries, Chinese vegetable dishes, and broiled fish, but take care until you adjust to the new flavor.

Seeds are great when ground and sprinkled in soups, stuffing, and sauces for meat dishes.

HINTS FOR FEBRUARY

Bring in forsythia and pussy willows for forcing.

Last call for seed orders.

Last call for plant orders.

Check your held-over fuchsias: Do they need water?

Examine the garden for mouse or rabbit damage. Either repair fences or cry a lot.

It's time to start seeds for perennials.

For an afternoon's project, build an electric seedbed.

Keep a record of everything that you order.

As the days become longer and soil in pots begins to warm, watch for the emergence of insect pests.

Make sure you order enough potting medium and peat pots for starting seeds.

Check your emergency heaters. Now is the time for ice storms in the Northeast and the power outages that follow.

Look to cactuses and succulents for a rewatering schedule.

Notes

[I] destroyed an old-fashioned garden. I doomed it and all its embellishments...to sudden and total destruction; probably much upon the same idea as many a man of careless, unreflecting, unfeeling good nature thought it his duty to vote for demolishing towns, provinces, and their inhabitants in America: like me they chose to admit it as a principle, that whatever obstructed the prevailing system must be all thrown down, all laid prostrate: no medium, no conciliatory methods were to be tried, but whatever might follow, destruction must proceed.

SIR UREDALE PRICE

Now that spring is in the wings and thoughts of winter's gloom seem to recede from view, it's time to ready for another year in the garden and the great outdoors. Unfortunately, it's also time for the prime movers to gear up their machinery for another forceful assault on the land still open to fields, still covered with woods.

If you are interested in wild gardens that could feature the flowers that abound in field and forest, keep your eyes open for the developer and his machines; you might be able to rescue an endangered species or a little-known fern before it's buried under a ton of mediocre planning. To be on the safe side, always ask permission. You might be branded a conservationist, but there are worse things to be called.

THE KAFFIR LILY

Ten years ago this month I bought a plant by mail: a puny thing with two straplike leaves and three white roots in a plastic pot, all wrapped with polyethylene and doubled over from a two-week transit in the even-then-deteriorating postal service.

The plant was called a Kaffir lily or *Clivia miniata* (pictured at left), named after one of the duchesses of Northumberland who was born a Clive and died back in 1866. A member of the amaryllis family, the Kaffirs consist of a radial growth of thick leaves (from one to two feet in length), are tropical, evergreen, and make perfect houseplants, especially since they tolerate temperatures from 50°F. up.

Three years passed while my plant added a few leaves and struggled to fill a four-inch pot. Then *voilà!* It began to take off and threw out leaf after leaf, soon splitting asunder a five-inch, then a six-inch pot, winding up (for now) in an eight-inch plastic container that is beginning to warp from the pressure of expanding roots.

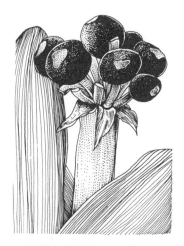

CLIVIA SEEDS

Clivia blossoms will go to seed and form green pods that ripen to red berries containing viable seed. Use only fresh seed and supply bottom heat of 70°F. for germination, which occurs in about six to eight weeks. Plants should come into bloom approximately two years after germination, with seedlings potted up in three-inch pots.

Every spring, at the end of February and to the middle of March, the flowers appear: large, funnel-shaped, with throats of the brightest yellow shifting to the brightest of oranges at petal's tip, twelve to twenty blooms clustered atop a thickened and flattened stem. A spectacular plant and worthy of being in every plant collection.

They rest most of the winter, wanting neither too much heat nor light, and no water at all (except to keep the soil from blowing away). After flowering is over, they require copious amounts of water and, if potbound, a good deal of fertilizer.

Kaffirs succeed best in a good loam with some leafmold and charcoal added. They need repotting only when they burst the sides of their present homes; an annual topdressing of fresh soil is usually enough.

Propagate from seeds or by dividing the new plants that appear about the base of the parent plant.

The seedpods will hang upon the plant all winter and are decorative in their own right. There are now many different varieties of this plant being offered, including a stunning variegated type.

These plants need good light, but protect them from summer sun if left outside in the garden for a vacation from the house.

THE LURE OF THE ARBOR

Among the more pleasant memories of my childhood — memories that have a tendency to resurface as the years roll by — are the afternoons spent in my mother's garden during the carefree days of summer vacation after grade school recessed. Those were the days of polio epidemics, and since our yard was large and bordered on a pine woods, most of the neighborhood gang was cloistered there. For those too young to remember, the idea was to keep all the children from one neighborhood together and truly ostracize any outsiders, thus isolating any infections — and it seemed to work.

About noon my mother would appear with trays of peanut-butter-and-jelly sandwiches, sliced carrots, one hard-boiled egg apiece, some peanuts, celery sticks, and large glasses of cold milk, glasses streaked with sweat from the summer heat.

Everyone would head for the arbor: the white wooden arches towered above our heads, and almost every conceivable spot was festooned with a huge and flowering clematis. It was not as large as memory serves, standing no more than eight feet high at the center, but size is a relative thing in the mind's eye of a child.

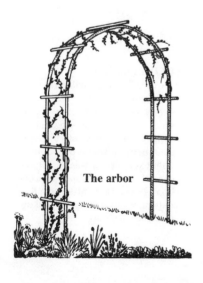

The arbor

Two benches, one on each side of the arbor, provided seats for only six kids; one child always had to sit on the grass in the center, determined by drawing the shortest stick of celery. But the best vantage point was on the ground, for the blossoms were more mysterious when touched with shade and the insects decidedly more interesting about the roots.

This all leads to the news that you can now have an arbor — not of wood, but made from strong steel tubes that are weatherproofed with a natural looking green plastic and fit together like soda straws from milk shakes of yore. Over eight feet tall and five feet wide, such an arbor could easily become the focal point of any garden. The lightweight frame cannot rot, splinter, or harbor insects; it seems built for a lifetime of use.

Instructions say to glue the joints, but hold off until you are sure of staying where you are; this is one garden accessory you will want to take wherever you go!

CHINESE CHIVES

A few years ago a friend in California sent us a package of Chinese chive seeds *(Allium tuberosum)* called *gow choy* by the Chinese. She told us to start them indoors in late March just like regular chives, but to be prepared for a surprise. We planted them outside in May and by late July the foot-high chive leaves were topped with bunches of delicate white, star-shaped flowers, entirely unlike the purple gloves of regular chives. She instructed us to chop up the budding flower stalks and add them to salad. They were wonderful! The buds have a mild and pleasant garlic taste while the leaves incline to that of onions.

When fall arrived, we potted up a few of the plants in six-inch clay pots where they produced enough leaves to brighten many a winter salad. When the leaves begin to dry, the plant needs a rest but can be brought back to life by warming up the surrounding temperatures and adding water.

It is no exaggeration to say that these plants should be in every flower garden, for those blossoms left to form seed produce straw-colored dried flowers dotted with coal-black seeds.

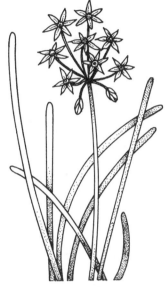

Chinese chives

CYMBIDIUM ORCHIDS

There was a time when orchids were thought to be rich people's playthings—luxury blooms that demanded greenhouse care and a staff of horticulturists and flower arrangers of infinite taste to bring out the best of their blooms. Frankly, with the rising costs of home heating, many of the more popular varieties *are* expensive pursuits and, in my opinion, are rather ugly flowers on ugly plants.

Cymbidiums, however, are orchids of a different color; they stand relatively alone as undemanding orchids that repay an owner's modicum of care with a burst of blooms appearing between late February and June and lasting well over one month. Even when not in flower, the long, graceful leaves are an attractive feature.

Cymbidiums do well in a good potting soil mixed with peat moss, enjoying a dash of fertilizer once a month during the summer. They tolerate temperatures as low as 40°F., but not for more than two or three weeks at a time, preferring 45°–55°F. as the winter norm, and need the diminished light of winter coupled with a reduction in watering in order to instigate blooming.

When spring blooming is over and there is no fear of frost, move the plants outside into the sun or set them in a sunny window. The

CYMBIDIUMS IN BLOOM

The drawing on the previous pages shows a pot of cymbidiums (*Cymbidium* × 'San Francisco'), a beautiful pink corsage flower, that have bloomed every year since I acquired them in 1975. Each individual blossom can be plucked from the stem, wrapped in a small piece of damp tissue paper, then with a bit of aluminum foil, to become a charming corsage. A whole stem can be cut at the base (use a clean knife) and kept in a bowl of water if you have no room on the table for a complete plant.

Japanese sedge grass

higher temperatures and sunlight will provoke the plants into setting buds for the next season. Don't forget to give them plenty of water during this time; I am very free and easy with the garden hose, misting and watering well every other day, more when days are very hot. In latitudes below New York, give some protection from the noonday sun of July and August.

When roots grow to such an extent that plants start to rise out of the pot, it's time to divide in half and repot in at least a six-inch pot.

THE UBIQUITOUS SEDGE

Today is one of those early March days when everything you see is best exemplified by Rita Hayworth's remark to Jack Lemmon in *Fire Down Below:* "Armies have marched over me!" Even the snow deep within the northern woods, where air pollution never goes, has a used and smutty look.

Determined to find a symbol of better times to come, I went for a walk in the garden and saw my Japanese sedge grass *(Carex Morrowii* var. *expallida)* appearing beneath the melting snow. Some leaves had been burned by the low temperatures of late fall, but others were still healthy and glowing with color, truly evergreen in character.

Sedges are members of a large group of plants that greatly resemble grasses but have a family of their own. Sometimes the differences are hard to discern, but usually the stems of sedges are triangular in cross section while grass stems are round. Sedge stems are filled with a white, pithy substance that was once used to make candle wicks or candles by soaking in kitchen grease.

On an economic scale of one to ten, most people would rate the sedge a generous -50, but for decorative purposes they excel. The gracefully arched leaves of the Japanese sedge are striped with creamy white and yellow-green, usually reaching a length of six to ten inches and forming a mound of leaves up to a foot high.

As a pot plant, Japanese sedge is a good choice as long as you keep it in a cool place and use a soil mix of potting soil, peat moss, and sand, one-third of each. Give the plant plenty of winter light and it will generally bloom in early spring—unresplendent flowers that resemble small camel's hair brushes dipped in golden pollen.

In the garden they prefer a shaded spot in moist soil. From zone 4 on north, give them protection if snow cover is absent from your region.

GARDEN VERSE

Although the days are noticeably longer, spring and summer are still weeks away, but the garden mood can be intensified by reading garden verse. After checking the index references to gardens in the *Oxford Dictionary of Quotations,* I found the following from Kipling's *Glory of the Garden,* and though it hovers slightly above the level of verse found on greeting cards—those that cost $1 as opposed to the 25¢ type—there is inherent truth within its lines:

...seek your job with thankfulness and
    work till further orders,
If it's only netting strawberries or
    killing slugs on borders;
And when your back stops aching and
    your hands begin to harden,
You will find yourself a partner in the
    Glory of the Garden.
Oh, Adam was a gardener, and God
    who made him sees
That half a proper gardener's work is
    done upon his knees,
So when your work is finished, you can
    wash your hands and pray
For the Glory of the Garden, that it may
    not pass away!

In fact, many of the lines would do well engraved about the edge of a sundial to replace the timeworn phrase "I count only happy hours."

The more romantic souls among us—I included—would most likely concur with Tennyson's call to Maud:

Come into the garden, Maud,
    For the black bat, night, has flown;
Come into the garden, Maud,
    I am here at the gate alone;
And the woodbine species are wafted abroad,
    And the musk of the rose is blown.

The entire poem, however, is vastly tinged with purple. I turn instead for the complete statement of the art to Thomas Edward Brown, who simply said: "A garden is a lovesome thing, god wot!" And in the same poem:

Not God! in gardens! when the eve is cool?
Nay, but I have a sign;
'Tis very sure God walks in mine.

And speaking of kneeling, allow me to mention that most afflicted portion of the gardener's anatomy, the knee. Obviously when the knee was designed, no thought was given to kneeling; or if it was, the assumption was to make it as uncomfortable as possible.

In addition, many of our best gardeners have occasion to be cursed with varying forms of rheumatism and arthritis, not to mention the problem confronting almost 80 percent of the American population: lower back pain.

For many seasons I've gathered my shovels, rakes, forks, trowels, barrows, and various other sundries, clothed my person in flannel shirt and dungarees, added a repellent for blackflies, gone to work in the garden, and been in pain within five minutes; for not only do dungarees soak up water, but the material holds any slight or tiny pebble and quickly works it into your knee.

I assume that most people have found a solution, but for those who, like me, must be hit over the head more than once to score a point, I advise that you use the following: foam or leather kneepads.

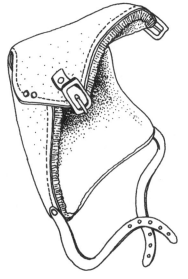

Kneepads

This is a book about flowers; vegetables are another matter entirely. But mention must be made of a few that transcend, and one prize is the leek.

I first encountered this delicacy of the onion family when on a trip to York, Pennsylvania, at the end of March some years ago. Their climate is much milder than ours and the rich farmlands that surround York are being worked while our garden is yet a sea of white.

While there, we wandered over to a large Quaker market—not its actual name but referred to by that term as most of the personnel are members of the Quaker faith—for shoofly pie, a cup of coffee, and to enjoy the sights and smells.

One booth was heaped high with giant onions. Well, not onions, but more like huge bunching onions or scallions, and many were well over two feet long. I asked what these strange members of the onion family were and the lady responded with "Leeks! They make the finest soup in the world!"

She told us how to prepare them: Wash carefully because the leaves that wrap the tender bulb have a tendency to pick up sand or soil particles as they grow (and even then you always miss a few) and remove the roots. Her other bit of advice was to always use fresh cream when preparing the soup.

We've enjoyed this super vegetable at many dinners since and grow them every year. Varieties to try are Yates Empire, Everest (one of the largest in existence), Marble Pillar (solid white stems up to 25 percent longer than any other variety), and the new Alaska (extremely hardy).

Just serve a cheese sauce on boiled or braised leeks and you will have a dish worth fighting for.

THE PERUVIAN SQUILL

The flower blooming on the left page is known as a Peruvian lily or squill but has nothing to do with that country, hailing instead from southern Europe and northern Africa. It's an excellent choice for growing in the window, where the numerous flower heads dance around a growing stem (or scape) and last for weeks.

The bulb is not hardy and should be potted in a well-drained soil with some compost added. Keep the pot in a cool place (50°F.) and water enough to keep the compost moist and the bulbs growing. They will bloom about two months after planting.

Keep them growing until the leaves die naturally, then rest the bulbs for a few months before starting again. Repot when the pot is full.

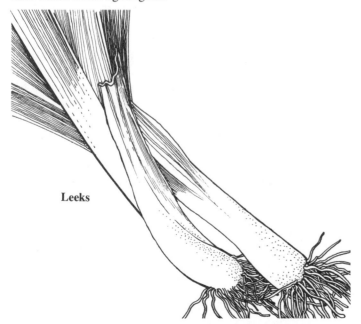

Leeks

Russian mustard

FREESIAS

Freesias are members of the iris family and hail from South Africa. Numerous fragrant and tubular flowers are borne at right angles to the flower scape and come in varying shades of white, yellow, rose, purple, and brown. They make excellent cut flowers.

A VERY EARLY SPRING

I am writing this on the afternoon of March 31, 1981. A warm wind is blowing and there's been a promise of rain since early in the morning. But there is a wrongness to the day; the warm air does not belong to trees that are barren of leaves, or to brown fields that are dashed with white—fields without the hum of bees or the whir of wings.

Out in the backyard, the yellow crocuses have been in bloom for over two weeks. In fact, their bright petals are already worn and torn from late-winter winds.

The snowdrops *(Galanthus nivalis)* that always bend their three-petaled heads to the ground are doing so with a greater fervor than usual; they are on familiar terms with snow and the chills of early spring, but today is much too warm and they begin to wilt.

On the top of the ridge behind the house, I've planted draba, or Russian mustard *(Draba lasiocarpa),* tiny plants from the arctic circle or the steppes of central Asia that are usually at home only on higher mountain peaks; they open their bright yellow, four-petaled blooms only after melting the surrounding snow with self-generated heat. No snow today, and they, too, seem exhausted by the air. Their usual sweet smell, so noticeable on chilly days, is missing this day. A few flies are there, but drawn by the bright color that sings against the background of gray stone and brown grass, not by perfume. The bees have yet to wake.

Tulip leaves are up. . .white forsythia buds are ready now to burst . . .lilac leaves are swelling with their fresh green peeking from the brown covers, and it's only just the end of winter. Imagine what the soft and gentle rains of spring will bring!

FREESIAS

I was introduced to freesias by the grower in one of our local greenhouses. On a bleak day in March, he was showing me their collection of Easter lilies, lined up in hundreds of pots and just starting to come into bud for the approaching holiday, when I noticed a rich, sweet aroma. We walked over to pots of very tall leaves and sprays and nodding waxy-yellow flowers. Most of his blooms had already been cut for floral bouquets, but the few that were left perfumed the entire greenhouse.

Freesias *(Freesia × hybrida)* are very easy to grow for winter bloom, the only requirement being a place where temperatures of 50°–55°F. can be maintained. If you intend growing them in a warm home or apartment, be sure that you buy precooled corms or have a friend with facilities to keep them between 45°F. and 50°F. for three to four weeks before you pot them up.

Plant six corms (a particular type of root that resembles a bulb but isn't) point-up in a six-inch pot of mixed peat moss and vermiculite. The corms should be about an inch below the level of the mix. Be careful to protect the husk that covers the surface. Water well and leave alone for about ten days. Keep the mix on the dry side, never soaking wet. As the leaves develop, stake the plants

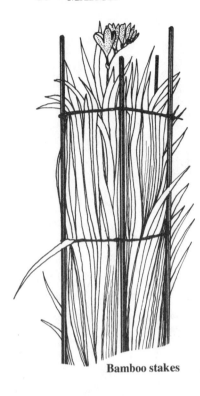

Bamboo stakes

with four bamboo canes and string (see illustration). They grow so tall that they will flop over if not held up. Give them maximum light for the best flower production.

The plants will bloom about four months after growth is initiated. After flowering, remove the dead blooms and allow the foliage to die back. Then put the pots aside for the summer and allow the corms to ripen and dry.

HINTS FOR MARCH

Check garden tools for use outside within a month.

Make sure that any perennials and shrubs that heave are pushed back into the ground.

Check your houseplants: See if they need to be moved to larger pots and get a new helping of fresh soil for the coming months of growth.

Check your garden hoses: Do they need repair or replacement?

Days are getting longer; it's time for your indoor plants to wake up. They will need more water and perhaps the leaves should be washed and dusted.

Seedlings can now be potted up. In the colder parts of the country, it's only eight weeks now until the last frost.

The Philadelphia Flower Show is this month.

The New England Flower Show is this month.

NOTES

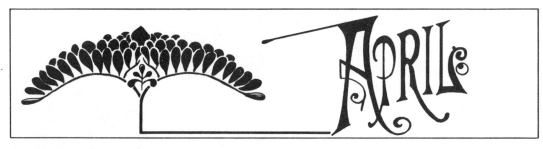

A man really in love with a garden is perhaps safer from the usual human temptations than any other... woman has no seductions for the man who cannot take his eyes from his magnolias.

A gentleman who is responsible for one of the cruellest wars in the history of the world is known to have a passion for orchids—though those who see something evil and abnormal in the orchid, in spite of its beauty, will perhaps see a certain fitness in his taste....

...steal out sometimes after sunset and walk up and down between the home end of the garden and the wild end and listen to the sounds at each....

R. LeGallienne in 1912

After one has been a gardener for a time, the urge to collect more than plants becomes apparent, and the plantsman* turns to books about gardening, books to while away the nonproductive hours far from the yard, to entertain the intellect, to bring pictures to the mind's eye.

The quotes at the beginning of this and some other chapters come from an old book entitled *Corners of Old Grey Gardens,* first published in 1914, residing for a time in an old New York bookstore, thence to the Garden Club of Cleveland as a gift, on to the Cleveland Garden Center, then deaccessioned and given freedom, and finally winding up in my care, tattered and torn, but charming and full of pleasures of the garden, a lifeline from one garden time to another.

Perhaps the woman of today would prefer not to be compared to a magnolia; I'm unable to fathom the name of the infamous warlord of pre-1914 who loved orchids; and there are parts of the book that will never live again. But, ah! The thoughts of the home end of the garden...

ROSEMARY FOR REMEMBRANCE

Rosemary *(Rosmarinus officinalis)* is an evergreen perennial with gray-green needlelike leaves and lavender flowers—like tiny elongated snapdragons—in spring. The plant is not hardy below 15°F., so in the North it must spend the winter indoors in a pot with reduced watering until April. Outside in warmer climates, rosemary can grow to the size of a small bush—six to seven feet high

A DISH GARDEN

The dish garden pictured at left consists of small cactuses and succulents that are happy in close quarters and will bloom every spring if given just a reasonable amount of care. Clockwise from the top right are: *Aloinopsis rosulata, Cotyledon orbiculata, Gymnocalycium Fidaianum, Pleiospilos bolusii, Fenestraria rhopalophylla,* and *Hatiora salicornioides.*

Cactuses and succulents have shallow root systems so a dish two and a half inches high makes a fine home for the plants shown. Use a soil mix of one-third good potting soil, one-third sharp (or builder's sand), and one-third composted cow manure, and set plants to a two-inch depth. To provide good drainage, place an inch or so of small pieces of broken pottery or small, clean stones to the dish bottom before sprinkling in the loose soil. Cool temperatures should prevail in winter (55°F) and hold back on watering unless the plants begin to shrivel. Full watering should begin in late winter when the days are once again longer; water whenever the soil becomes dry and use a dilute liquid plant food once a month in summer. They want bright light at all times but not necessarily full sun in July and August.

*"A *plantsman* is one who loves plants for their own sake," wrote Mr. David McClintock. "This concept may include a botanist: it certainly includes a host of admirable amateurs...." It is also a generic term, not sexist, and any gardener who wishes to be called a "plantsperson" gets exactly what he or she deserves.

with a spread of some six feet—but in the confines of a pot, it rarely tops three feet.

Use a standard potting soil cut almost in half with sharp sand; no rich diet here or the odor and flavor of the leaves will be markedly reduced.

Six-inch cuttings of the stem will easily root in moist sand with the bottom two-thirds under cover.

The young, freshly picked leaves are used in flavoring stews, fish and meat sauces, and sparsely in the preparation of salads. Its flavor also mixes well with lamb, and when fresh leaves are available, my wife adds them to scrambled eggs.

In ancient Greece, rosemary was thought to strengthen the brain and the memory and thus has become the symbol of remembrance.

THE ORCHID CACTUS

The orchid cactus *(Epiphyllum × hybridus)* looks handsome at any time of the year with its long, flat, straplike stems (and they *are* stems, for the leaves are reduced to tiny spines in this member of the succulent tribe), and the older the plant, the more architectural its look. But with the coming of spring, tiny buds appear between the scallops on the stem, buds that grow visibly larger every day until suddenly they open into truly breathtaking flowers. Colors are vibrant, and the texture of the petals resembles that of glistening satin.

In nature, epiphyllums hang from trees, rooting where the branch meets the trunk, so they are quite at home suspended in wire baskets lined with dried moss, in hanging clay or plastic pots, or merely standing on a flat surface with stems falling over a table's edge. Soil should be sandy and lean as a rich soil produces poor flowers.

Spray the plants with a mister during the warm days of spring and fall, withholding water from November through February (unless stems show signs of shriveling, at which time a dash of water is appreciated). During the summer months, hang the cactuses outdoors—under the shade of the porch eave or a tree—if you can. If the summer is unusually dry or the plant is sheltered from normal rains, you will have to water it, letting the soil dry out each time. Use plant food every three or four weeks in spring and summer.

To propagate, take four-inch cuttings, let them air-dry for a few days, then root in a mix of moist sphagnum or peat moss. They will usually root with ease.

When indoors, the orchid cactus will withstand temperatures of 45°F without ill effect, but keep from freezing as it is not hardy.

THE FABLED WHITE FORSYTHIA

When we first planned on landscaping our backyard and garden, the thought of forsythia crossed our minds but was quickly dismissed when the mind's eye saw visions of acre after acre of those yellow blooms on bending branches that represent the ultimate in creative gardening in most of the country, No, we said, to forsythia (and to crown vetch, which threatens to overtake most of the

Rosemary

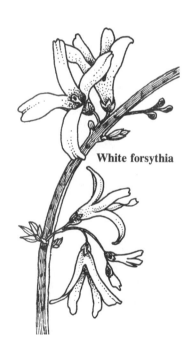

White forsythia

THE ORCHID CACTUS
The plant on the previous page is an orchid cactus *(Epiphyllum × hybridus)* that blooms every year with a minimum of care.

Pennsylvania highway system; and no to the mighty kudzu vine that is busily engaged in devouring the South).

Then we noticed a catalog entry devoted to *Abeliophyllum distichum,* or white forsythia, a singular genus with one species found in Korea in 1924 and first imported to the United States by the White Flower Farm in 1955. The catalog claimed it to be hardy to zone 4, and we tried one plant in 1979.

Every year about the first week of April, the bush begins to bloom. At first the four petals are suffused with pink, but as they open the pink fades to a perfect white, The entire bush — now six feet tall and planning to grow to seven—is covered with the flowers, and the corner where the bush grows is perfumed with a honeylike fragrance.

The buds become visible by late summer, dotting the branches with small bits of brown, and seem impervious to the worst winds of winter. If you cannot wait for spring, branches cut in late winter can easily be forced into bloom.

This shrub will spread to some seven feet in diameter, and the arching branches covered with bluish-green leaves make it a desirable small addition to almost any garden. Average soil will do fine.

A VERY DELICATE BLUE

Count Apollos Apollosovich Mussin-Puschkin (1760–1805) left Russia in the year 1800 for the loftier regions of the Caucasus in search of mineral wealth — the first Russian to take a portable laboratory into the field for on-the-spot assays — and died in the mountains after mentioning that the plague was particularly bad that season, especially among members of the expedition.

He had written to Sir Joseph Banks in England and offered to send seeds and natural-history specimens in return for seeds of American trees that he hoped to naturalize in the mountains. I have no idea what American plants he introduced to the Caucasus or what mineral wealth he found for the czar, but I do know of one flowering bulb that the count introduced to the gardeners of the world: the striped squill, or *Puschkinia scilloides.* The genus has only two species, both bearing a few flowers—sometimes just one —on a short stem. They bloom from mid- to late April in zone 5 and the count could have no finer namesake.

Flowers resemble hyacinths, but where the hyacinth stem is crowded with big and vulgar flowers, drenched with powerful perfumes, puschkinias are a delicate white with just a hint of pastel blue, each petal bearing one pale blue stripe—nothing vulgar here.

Stems rarely reach above six inches and the only requirement is that soil be of a reasonably well-drained nature, easily accomplished by adding sand to the existing soil or planting the bulbs in a rock-garden format.

Once planted, the bulbs naturalize with ease; seeds are produced, and many germinate on the spot. No, it never becomes a pest as the leaves are gone by the end of May. Plants are extremely hardy.

Order them now for fall planting. If you can find it, the white form, **'Alba'** is lovely.

Puschkinia scilloides

I wandered lonely as a cloud
  That floats on high o'er vales and hills,
When all at once I saw a crowd,
  A host of golden daffodils;
Beside the lake, beneath the trees,
  Fluttering and dancing in the breeze.

The words of William Wordsworth are best read as you look out of your window toward the garden and spy the daffodils and narcissus that you planted the previous fall.

Daffodils naturalize with ease and spread over almost any terrain except waterlogged soil or solid rock and clay. They need a sunny spot in spring but do not object to a slight bit of shade as tree leaves develop; even the midst of your lawn is a good spot as long as you don't cut the grass until after the leaves have withered and browned, allowing the bulbs to store for next year's blooming.

Many of the smaller species are at home in the rock garden, and a few like *Narcissus Bulbocodium* and *N. calcicola* will do well in pots of well-drained soil if given very cool growing conditions in a greenhouse.

For instructions on naturalizing these flowers of spring, see p. 105 in September's chapter.

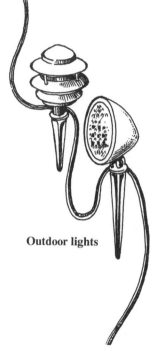

Outdoor lights

OUTDOOR LIGHTING

There is another dimension to the garden today and it's called "low-voltage lighting." Using a transformer to change the regular household current of 120 volts to a safe 12-volt system, your backyard and garden can be aglow with lights with a system that is so safe that children and pets—and you—are completely safe from shock even if installing the system in a rainstorm.

Low-voltage lamps are used in conjunction with a special, flexible power cable that you can bury right under the surface of the ground with a simple trowel as a tool. Small lamps sit directly on the ground ready to light your garden path, and small floodlights can be fixed to tree branches, bathing leaves with white or, if you prefer, colored lights. After the sun goes down, the garden is a more magical place than ever before.

Each system of lights, receptacles, and transformer should not be over 100 feet in length and should be limited to eight lamps.

If there is magic in the summer garden, the lights that twinkle during a snowstorm, when viewed from a cozy interior, add yet another dimension to your yard.

A guardian owl

GUARDING THE GARDEN

With the coming of spring and the waking of the garden, animal pests again become a problem. Here is one solution, the great horned owl. Made of inflatable plastic, the owl should be mounted on top of a stake or in a tree overlooking the garden. Inflation should be checked periodically as a flaccid owl is hardly any threat. The manufacturer advises that the owl be moved every few days to prevent rabbits, rodents, and other birds from getting used to it.

THE NARCISSUS

These flowers are called "narcissus" when the central cup or eye is small and "daffodils" when the cup becomes a trumpet, yet they all belong to the *Narcissus* genus. They range in size from the very large daffodil at right, *Narcissus* 'Foresight', with petals of white and a yellow trumpet, to the diminutive narcissus below, *N. juncifolius,* happier at home in a rock garden than on the side of a hill.

One of my favorite plants came to me from a fan in the Azores. Thinking that our winters were as mild as hers, she sent me a CARE package of various plants that unfortunately arrived in the middle of December. Of course, all the plants were dead except one poor orchid without identification, brown and shriveled but showing a touch of green beneath the damaged tissue.

I recognized it as a cymbidium from the general structure and the shape of the dead leaves (see p. 29 in the March chapter) and planted it in a porous soil mix. The year was 1975.

By 1980, the orchid looked like a healthy specimen: four pseudo-bulbs held a good percentage of foliage, and leaves were about two feet long. Then in early March a flower spike appeared. Every morning the spike grew longer until, on the morning of April 16, a total of thirty buds were in evidence and the first of them began to open.

I recognized it immediately as a *Cymbidium Lowianum,* not because of any great orchid knowledge on my part but because it is so often pictured in orchid books, where it is described as originating in the mountains of Burma, and important as the jumping-off plant in experiments with cymbidium hybridization.

I'm still elated. It took only six years and proves that gardeners, in addition to their many other virtues, are a patient lot.

WILLOW WREATHS FOR SPRING

A very old and charming custom in the country revolves around the making of wreaths to celebrate the coming of spring. Long yellow branches of the weeping willow tree are cut with a sharp knife or shears, woven into a circular wreath, and decorated with sprigs of dried pussywillows and forsythia blossoms.

Additional wreaths can be made from grapevines cut throughout the year, although October through April is the best time for harvest. These vines must be soaked in hot water to make them pliable, then follow the instructions for the willow wreath.

SHOPPING BY MAIL

The following quote is taken from the April 1882 issue of the *Ladies' Floral Cabinet,* a news magazine published for women:

> **This is the busy season for the gardeners, if they would have everything in fine order for the summer . . . All lovers of flowers who live remote from city markets have reason to thank the Post Office Department, whose daily mail-bags come laden with packages of plants and bundles of seeds of every description, from the Atlantic coast to the Pacific slope, and give to those who live at the most remote points the same advantages as to those who live near the large plant centres.**

Well, that was 1882! The last 100 years has seen a change in the old post office. No longer do plants arrive safely in the mail; more often than not, they are damaged beyond repair. But fear not! Most

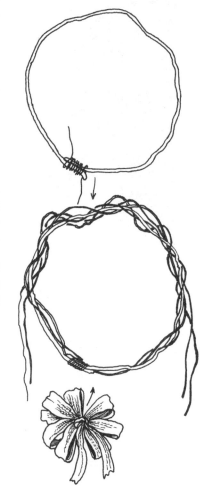

Start with a long, thick branch, looped and tied. Wrap other branches around the base in spiral fashion. Tie the ends with string, which is removed when the wreath dries to shape.

nursery suppliers of today use commercial package shippers, like United Parcel, and plants are now shipped with their root balls intact, well wrapped, and guaranteed to survive.

VENUS'S-FLYTRAP

Certain plants are always in the forefront of the public eye, often because they are simply beautiful, come from exotic climes, or have a reputation for horror. Venus's-flytrap represents horror.

It's the best-known of all the insectivorous plants, conjuring up images of giant and vicious jaws snapping shut on hapless ladies dressed in sarongs while foraging the Amazon jungles for lost treasures, lost friends, or black orchids. In truth a rather small plant, not equipped for devouring maidens, it's a fascinating specimen.

Found only in North and South Carolina bogs, Venus's-flytrap (*Dionaea muscipula*) was first discovered by Governor Arthur Dobbs of North Carolina in 1759. Governor Dobbs published the following description: "...The great wonder of the vegetable kingdom is a very dwarf plant...leaves are like a narrow segment of a sphere, consisting of two parts, like the cap of a spring purse, the concave part outward, each of which falls back with indented edges (like an iron spring fox trap); upon anything touching the leaves, or falling between them, they instantly close like a spring trap...It bears a white flower; to this surprising plant I have given the name of Flytrap Sensitive."

I've yet to discover who thought of adding "Venus," but it must have been an eighteenth-century misogynist.

The traps are green in poorer light and turn a deep crimson as the intensity of light increases. The surface of each trap has three hairs that respond to touch and close the trap. The time needed to snap shut can be several seconds or less than one-half second, depending on the age of the individual trap and the temperature. The trap will reopen within a day if fooled by a broomstraw or a matchstick. If it does catch a meal, it's digested in four to twenty days, depending on the size of the victim. Signal hairs must be touched twice within about twenty seconds or the trap will not close, probably to prove to the leaf that it has a live meal.

Like all other insectivores, these plants must have warmth, light, and high humidity, with a dormant resting period during the winter months. The older the bulb, the larger the trap.

April is the best time to buy and start the bulbs. Happy plants will reward the grower with small, white wavy-edged flowers that are both dainty and attractive.

It's an interesting addition to the home garden, but if you plan to replace flyswatters or insecticides, forget it.

After a few meals or with increasing age, the traps turn black. Snip them off and new traps will grow.

REPOTTING PLANTS

When a plant needs repotting, it's only moved up one pot size, or, at the most, two. A small plant in a large pot not only looks strange, it usually doesn't last too long. Unless roots extend throughout most

Venus's-flytrap

of the soil, the excess becomes soggy and compacted, leading to sickly growth.

Repotting becomes necessary when the roots completely occupy all of the soil and the root ball assumes the shape of the pot. The first signs are roots working their way through the drainage hole. The best time for repotting is very early spring or late winter when plants are just beginning active growth after months of rest. The worst time is in December or January when roots are truly inactive and, if broken during repotting, become possible victims of disease. Of course, actively growing plants can be repotted at any time.

If you are worried about a plant being potbound, you can easily check by placing a finger on each side of the stem to hold the root ball and flipping the pot over. Rap it sharply on a table edge and the soil ball should slide out. Wait until the soil is dry for this routine as wet soil will fight you all the way.

If all looks okay and roots are not massed on the outside of the soil, pop the plant back into the pot. If not, repot in the next-larger-size pot.

One important thing to remember: Leave enough room at the top of the pot for watering. With a five-inch pot, there should be at least a three-quarter-inch clearance between the rim and the soil surface. Nothing can be as aggravating as watering a plant, dribbling mud down the pot's outside, then having to go at it again because in the first attempt the plant got half and the floor got the rest.

After potting, water the plant well to help settle the soil. If you packed it a bit on the loose side, you will note a few depressions. Just sprinkle some more soil in them to level the surface. I always add a small shard or flat stone to break the force of water when watering.

LABELS FOR THE GARDEN

Every spring when I go out into the garden, I see a conglomeration of broken plastic bits or splintered chips of wood lying about the barren ground, all that is left of my noble efforts at providing labels for the garden plants I wish to remember. For regardless of the stalwart cries of the plastic industry, most of their labels are puny things meant only for warmer climes and unable to withstand the rigors of a northern winter.

So every winter I attempt to mend my ways and seek out a better system. After years of research, I list the following types of more-permanent labels now available from a number of supply houses.

1. A white plastic type that is tied by a bit of wire to the plant stem rather than stuck into the ground.

2. A wooden label that is first soaked in wood preservative (don't use anything with creosote as it is poisonous to plants) and then has the plant name applied with paint, after which the wood is given two coats of a plastic finish.

3. A wooden dowel that is dipped into wood preservative then fitted with the brass screen numbers once

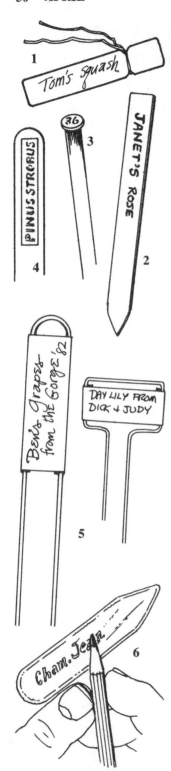

used as codes for old houses when matching a particular screen or storm window to a particular window. The system of numbers can be doubled or tripled by staining the dowels with different colors.

4. A wooden label with the plant name (or code number) printed by a label maker—preferably the type that uses stainless-steel or aluminum tape — glued to the tag.

5. A wire frame that holds pieces of lead sheeting that are inscribed with crayon or paint; the frames are long enough to withstand the heaving effects of frost.

6. Finally, a thin aluminum label inscribed with a pencil or ballpoint pen so that the ensuing indentations last many seasons.

HINTS FOR APRIL

Remove the mulch from roses, and prune winter damage.

Divide your ornamental grasses.

Plants will arrive by UPS; if you won't be home, make arrangements for someone to care for them until you return.

Don't forget to water seedlings; they dry out very quickly with the longer days and the hotter sun.

The rock garden should be in full bloom by now.

Don't be lulled by warm days; a frost can quickly appear.

Clean the lawn mower.

Remember to water any transplants, especially trees and shrubs.

Believe it or not, now is the time to start weeding.

Replace any labels that have broken or become indecipherable over the winter months.

Order your Japanese-beetle traps now; don't wait until the store is out of them.

After dividing perennials, trade some with gardening friends.

NOTES

When I walk out of my house into my garden I walk out of my habitual self, my every-day thoughts, my customariness of joy or sorrow by which I recognise and assure myself of my own identity. These I leave behind me for a time, as the bather leaves his garments on the beach.

...like a wise man, I am content with what I have, and make it richer by my fancy, which is as cheap as sunlight, and gilds objects quite as prettily. It is the coins in my pocket, not the coins in the pockets of my neighbor, that are of use to me.

ALEXANDER SMITH

May and June. Soft syllables, gentle names for the two best months in the garden year: cool, misty mornings gently burned away with a warming spring sun, followed by breezy afternoons and chilly nights. The discussion of philosophy is over, it's time for work to begin....

THE ROCK GARDEN

Rock gardens were originally designed for English gardeners to grow alpine and high-meadow plants from the mountains of Europe and Asia. They were the result of monumental labors in moving soil and rock, installing drains, digging ditches, and planning ahead for years.

Today's gardeners have no such labor force and rarely the room, hence trough gardenings (see p. 64) and the aboveground bed.

Since my backyard was made of red shale with a cover of pure clay, I decided that for growing rock garden plants, which need perfect drainage, I would build a fieldstone wall in the corner of the yard and fill it with rubble, gravel, peat moss, and composted manure, resulting in an enormous container as outlined in the following drawing:

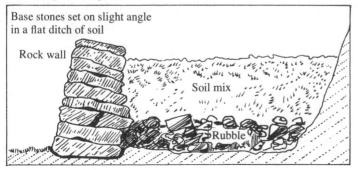

Base stones set on slight angle in a flat ditch of soil

Rock wall

Soil mix

Rubble

THE SALMON BLOOD LILY

Blood lilies are African bulbs grown for their fantastic flowers. The showy blooms—up to 100 individual flowers—form a perfect six- to seven-inch ball, each flower sending out six brilliant red stamens topped with bright yellow pollen for a total of 600. The salmon blood lily (*Haemanthus multiflorus*) will bloom in May or June.

Bulbs (which are up to three inches in diameter) should be potted in six- to eight-inch pots in a good soil mix that includes compost or manure. They need a winter rest (50–55°F.) and will bloom in the spring, the flowers appearing before the foliage. Keep the soil moist until leaves start to yellow, then dry off and restart growth the following spring. From May to August, give them a monthly dash of liquid plant food. Bulbs should be left undisturbed until they outgrow their pots.

53

(5)

(6)

(7)

(8)

The following eight plants are particularly suited for the rock garden as they are small in scale and need adequate drainage. If unable to construct a rock garden, try growing these flowers in a trough.

(1) Leopard's-bane *(Doronicum cordatum)* grows in a small clump and blooms in early summer or late spring. The daisies are a bright golden yellow.

(2) The Greek forget-me-not *(Omphalodes linifolia)* is an annual producing long sprays of lovely white, five-petaled flowers and more than enough seeds to keep both family and friends in supply.

(3) The alpine poppy *(Papaver alpinum)* is an annual or biennial depending on the climate where you garden. It will easily self-sow while never becoming a pest. This charmer will resist transplanting as its taproot is quite long and very quick-growing. Blossoms come in white, yellow, orange, and orange-red and have a very sweet and delicate fragrance.

(4) Aubrietas form mats of brilliant, starlike flowers in varying shades of blues and purples. *Aubrieta deltoidea* **'Dr. Mules'** is a very attractive cultivar. Plants are easily grown from cuttings or seed and if given a favorable spot in full sun will soon cover large areas of ground, especially happy on stone walls and abutments.

(5) *Ophiopogon planiscapus* **'Arabicus'** is a member of the lily family but not necessarily grown for flowers; rather, it's the striking dark purple, almost black color of the leaves that makes it a fine addition to the garden.

(6) The geranium pictured is a diminutive form of the bloody cranesbill, a wildflower from Europe and England *(Geranium sanguineum* var. *prostratum).* These are not the same plants as the popular bedding geraniums, which are correctly termed pelargoniums. These flowers like full sun, and old blossoms should be cut off to encourage more buds. Propagation is by division.

The pinks in the drawing are mat-forming perennials that are crowded with fragrant and spicy-scented five-petaled flowers in early spring. (7) *Dianthus Noeanus* bears fringed flowers of white, while (8) *D. alpinus* has larger blossoms of pale pink to light purple, depending on the plant. Seeds germinate with ease and often self-sow.

We are now going into the fourth year with this particular part of the garden. Since the underlying stones of the wall were set in with care, there has been a minimum of shifting. As the average fieldstone used was one and one-half to two feet wide and four to six inches thick, the wall has great stability; one can sit on the edge with comfort and look at smaller plants just below eye level.

THE ROCK GARDEN

The drawings on the previous pages show a rock garden in bloom. Individual plants are keyed to the text with the numerals.

GYPSY MOTHS AND TERMITES

With the charms of spring come the horrors of the insect war: gypsy moths and termites. Moths threaten most of the trees in America, and termites take care of house and garage foundations.

If you have moths, contact your local Cooperative Extension office and find out if there are any plans to spray your area.

Meanwhile, the following mechanical aids can help in controlling this pest:

Wrap pieces of burlap around trees needing protection, creating a shady trap for the caterpillars; remove them from the burlap every day or they will return to the treetops at night.

Sticky materials such as Tree Tanglefoot® may be used to band and protect a tree, but these glues may be harmful to young, thin-barked trees and should never be applied directly to the trunks but only over a nonporous material that is then wrapped around the tree.

After caterpillars reach one and one-half inches in length, it's too late for effective control with insecticides. There are traps that use pheromones to attract the male gypsy moth, but there are so many of these pests that your effort will go unrewarded. Instead, wait until late August, when the egg masses laid by the female moth will be visible, and scrape them off into a can and burn them.

Subterranean termites are a serious threat to your home because they eat away at wood without producing holes and sawdust as evidence of their presence. They are usually discovered in the following ways: (1) mud tunnels along the foundation of the house; (2) swarms of termites in the spring; (3) your wood joists and beams collapse; or (4) during structural alterations the damage is seen. If you find termites, call a commercial pest-control outfit.

LANTANA

Lantana

A basket plant that has been grown for years on the front porches of America is lantana *(Lantana camera)*. The flowers are yellow when they open, turn orange and then red, with all three colors being evident in the same flower. If flowers are not clipped off after bloom, small black berries may develop. Pinch back the stem tips for bushy growth.

Lantanas flower throughout the summer, enjoying full sun and warm temperatures (70°F.). The soil should be allowed to dry out between waterings.

Probably the most exciting thing about lantanas is turning a plant into a tree. Buy a small plant, preferably with only one main shoot, and pot it in a three-inch pot, and tie the stem to a foot-long bamboo cane or stick that you have inserted in the dirt at the pot's edge. Use one loop of soft cord about the stem and one loop on the stake so the stem is never crushed. When the lantana grows to about ten inches, move it to a six-inch pot, adding a longer length of stake (up to thirty inches). Now remove all the side shoots, leaving just one at the tip of the stem.

As the lantana approaches two feet, move it to an eight-inch pot. (Remember, all the time you've been forcing the plant upward, roots have been growing, too.) Now pinch off the terminal bud and new side shoots will appear. In turn, pinch off each of their terminal buds to force the plant into bushy growth. The stem will develop a woody look and you will have a beautiful flowering tree. The process may take up to two years, but you are creating an heirloom.

As the tree grows, it can be moved into bigger pots. Topdress the soil and fertilize during the summer months. Up north, lantanas will drop their leaves and enter a dormant period but will leaf out anew every spring. If you start your project this month, you will have a head start on next year.

WILDFLOWERS FOR THE GARDEN

The following pages describe nine beautiful wildflowers that will bring beauty to your perennial garden year after year with a minimum of effort on your part. Five of them prefer shade; the other four revel in full sun. Cultural requirements are given for each plant.

Wildflowers for a Shady Spot

Wild geranium *(Geranium maculatum):* These are late-spring bloomers with lavender-purple to pink flowers (occasionally white) on twelve- to eighteen-inch stems. They prefer a slightly damp spot with some organic matter in the soil and will bloom more profusely if given some morning sun. Propagation is by division in spring and they will also self-sow. Bunchberry *(Cornus canadensis):* A diminutive member of the dogwood family, bunchberry makes an effective ground cover in the shade. They grow just a few inches high from underground runners; preferring an acid soil in a cool and moist spot. They bloom in late spring. Propagation is by division of the runners and by planting the seeds that develop from berries in the fall. (1), (3)

Bead-lily *(Clintonia umbellulata):* This flower also enjoys a cool and shady spot with moderately acid soil of a loose and organic texture. Flowers are white on long stems that arise from a basal rosette of leaves, and eventually produce black berries. Plants are formed on underground runners and propagation is by seed or buying plants from specialty nurseries with the facilities to grow new plants from root divisions. (2)

Shooting star *(Dodecatheon meadia):* A beautiful late-spring flower with reflexed petals that resemble tiny rockets of pink or white. It prefers well-drained, slightly acid soil with partial shade (morning or evening sun). The plant should be mulched and its position well marked as leaves disappear shortly after flowers go to seed. Propagation is by division or seeds. (4)

Wintergreen *(Gaultheria procumbens):* These creepers form a six-inch-high mat of small evergreen leaves, blooming in early summer with tiny white bell-shaped flowers that are followed by larger red berries. Birds love them. Partial shade is needed and an acid and humusy soil, slightly moist. Propagation is by division of the rootstock. (5)

Wildflowers for a Sunny Spot

Blue dogbane *(Amsonia Tabernaemontana):* In a sunny spot with just about any soil, this plant produces terminal clusters of beautiful soft blue star-shaped flowers on stems up to three feet tall. With time a bushy clump is produced, so place this beauty with care.

WILDFLOWERS

The drawings on the next two pages are identified with the text by the key below:

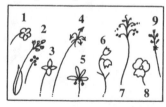

Leaves will turn yellow in the fall and the blooming period can be extended by removing dead flowers. Propagation is by division of a mature clump of plants. My plants have been subjected to −30°F. in our mountain winters, and they are perfectly hardy in zone 5. (9)

Mariposa lily *(Calochortus venustus):* This is a magnificent plant and the only one in the list that could present problems. It must have perfect drainage as the plant needs a dry summer and fall in order to bloom the following year. It needs mulching in any area without adequate snowfall, and must have sun at all times. Blooming is in early summer and the flowers are so beautiful that almost any effort to succeed with mariposa lily is rewarded. (8)

Harebell *(Campanula rotundifolia):* Small blue bells nod on foot-long wiry stems during the summer months. The plants need well-drained soil with full sun but must have water during periods of extreme dryness. Propagation is by division in the spring; plants will self-sow when happy. (6)

Coralbells *(Heuchera sanguinea):* Many stunning garden plants have been developed from this, the original wild coralbells. Sprays of tiny bells in red, pink, or white dance on one- to two-foot stems in late spring and early summer. They enjoy any good, well-drained garden soil. Older plants tend to crowd themselves out so should be divided and replanted in early spring every few years. Since plants grow close to the soil surface, watch for winter heaving, especially when snow cover is lacking and you haven't mulched. Removing spent blossoms can prolong bloom. Look for the Bressingham hybrids in perennial catalogs as they have marvelous colors. (7)

CALADIUMS

What's pink or white or deep red, maroon, speckled green, or any combination of the above? Fancy-leaved caladiums, of course. Caladiums *(Caladium hortulanum)* are tropical American tuberous herbs perfect for massing in a shady garden spot, under a tree, on the north side of the patio, or in pots for the greenhouse or home. Their one weakness is sensitivity to cold. Never plant them outside until night temperatures go no lower than 55°–60°F., yet keep them out of direct sunlight during summer months or the foliage will be scorched and browned.

To start them in pots, use a good potting soil mixed with sharp sand and composted manure, one-third each. Plant the knobby side up in six-inch pots, covering the tubers with an inch of medium. The best starting temperatures are in the range of 80°F., so a heating cable is needed in the northern states.

Keep the soil moist at all times, syringing the leaves with warm water during hot dry periods of summer.

In the fall when the first frost kills the leaves, tubers should be dug and stored over winter in a warm (60°–65°F.), dry spot.

They will do very well as houseplants if kept growing most of the year in a warm, well-lighted spot with a short rest in the depth of winter.

(1)

(2)

(3)

(4)

(5)

Two particularly magnificent cultivars are **'Brandywine'** with foot-long leaves of a deep wine red edged with green, and **'Candidum'** with snowy-white leaves fully marked with a network of green veins.

CLOCHES FOR PROTECTION

Cloches (from the French *cloche* meaning bell and referring to the bell-shaped jars first used for frost protection) are an economical way to use glass or plastic sheets for protecting your garden treasures from the threat of a sudden frost during these cool nights of spring. The drawing below shows three types of cloche clips now available in America:

The Glass Barn-Cloche

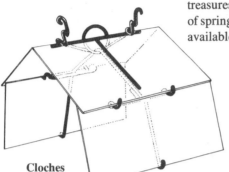

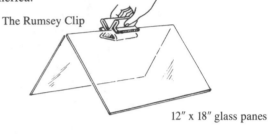

The Rumsey Clip

Cloches

12″ x 18″ glass panes

THE BLACK CAT

I really cannot testify to the effectiveness of *le chat noir,* the black cat, but the French claim that it's been scaring rabbits in their gardens for years. The eyes are clear glass marbles and glow in reflected light just like a real cat's will, and supposedly over 20 million are already in use. Called "effective, simple, humane, and silent" in the advertising, they are certainly worth a try and lead to comments by all visitors to the garden. Instructions advise moving them frequently and putting out several if you are protecting a large area. They are made of black-painted metal and should last for years.

The Royal Cloche Clip

CALADIUMS

The fancy-leaved caladium on the opposite page is growing in a six-inch pot in the shade of a weeping birch in our backyard garden. The strange hooded shape is the unusual flower that is sometimes seen blooming on a healthy plant. It resembles a jack-in-the-pulpit, to which it is closely related.

The black cat

THE TREE TOMATO

Cyphomandra betacea, the tree tomato, belongs to the same family as the garden-variety tomato and the potato. This fast-growing plant has been cultivated for centuries in Central and South America for its edible fruit, but outside of botanical gardens and a few knowledgeable growers in this country, tree tomatoes are relatively unknown.

It's a soft-wooded bush that grows to a height of ten feet in the wild, but is considerably smaller in the confines of the home.

Start your plant from seed or purchase a small specimen from a plant supplier. The tree tomato needs a good soil well-laced with organic matter or composted manure and should be repotted annually until it is at home in a large pot or small tub. If it gets too rangy, prune it in the spring, April or May.

Water well most of the year, holding back only in the midwinter months when light levels are low. Give plants plenty of sunlight and keep temperatures about 50°F. or above (though plants will survive an occasional dip to just above freezing). This plant is a good bet for the home as it does not enjoy high humidity levels.

The two-year-old plant pictured bloomed and bore fruit; I planted seed in the spring of 1980 and had flowers during the summer of 1982 followed by orangy-red, egg-shaped fruits about three inches long. Fruits start out green but continue to brighten as they ripen.

Recommended uses are as table fruit—they are said to be sweeter than the tomato—and as jam for bread and rolls. Unfortunately, the five fruits on my bush this year were not ready for personal testing by press time.

MAKING CONTAINERS FOR TROUGH GARDENING

If your garden has a limited amount of space or you wish to try growing some of the rarer and more difficult alpine plants without buying vast loads of sand, gravel, and soil to replace your backyard clay, you might consider trough gardens.

A trough is a special kind of container that originated on the farm as a feed or water trough or as the old-fashioned kitchen sink of the last few centuries. If you are fortunate enough to find an old soapstone sink, you will have a perfect aboveground container to start a small garden; or, if you live near one of the many nursery outlets that stock large concrete tubs for a reasonable price, you're ready to go.

But if you are without these lucky strikes, why not try making your own? You can do so using a mix of cement, sand, and peat moss that is called "hypertuffa" because of its resemblance to a naturally occurring porous stone called "tufa." By building wooden frames of varying dimensions, countless varieties of large pots, troughs, and tubs can be manufactured before you get involved with spring and the great outdoors.

Blend ingredients thoroughly. Gradually add water; the mix should be pliable, not runny. Let it sit for five minutes. Put a one-inch layer in the frame and set into the armature, an equal

THE TREE TOMATO
The tree tomato pictured at right bloomed and set fruit in its second year.

distance from all sides. Add more of the mix to make a one-and-a-half-inch layer all over the bottom, then set the inner frame in place. Set wooden plugs for drains. Fill the rest of the cavity and lay plastic over the top. In twelve to eighteen hours, remove the inner frame, carefully pulling out the side pieces, and remove the plugs. Replace the cover. Twenty-four hours later remove the outer form. Brush the sides and top to remove large bumps, but take care as the cement is still green. Wrap in plastic for three more days, clean the drainage holes, then leave it alone for at least another week while it fully hardens.

Now cure the trough (neutralize the cement) by filling it with water and adding one-half teaspoon of potassium permanganate crystals from the local drugstore. Using a paintbrush, coat the sides with the solution on the outside too. Let it sit for a few hours, then rinse well and let it sit in the weather for two more weeks before planting.

A good soil mix for the container would be equal parts of good garden loam or topsoil, well-rotted or composted manure, shredded peat moss, and builder's sand.

For more information on plants to grow in troughs, see the American Rock Garden Society listings in Appendix.

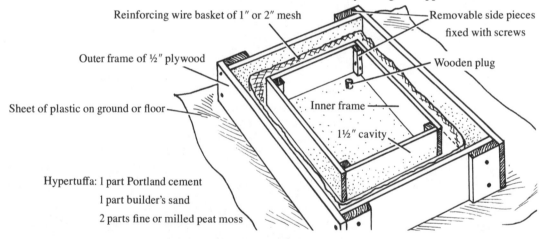

Reinforcing wire basket of 1″ or 2″ mesh

Removable side pieces fixed with screws

Outer frame of ½″ plywood

Wooden plug

Sheet of plastic on ground or floor

Inner frame

1½″ cavity

Hypertuffa: 1 part Portland cement
1 part builder's sand
2 parts fine or milled peat moss

HINTS FOR MAY

Take cuttings from your winter geraniums for the summer garden.

Get ready to plant summer bulbs like gladiolus.

Let the leaves of daffodils and narcissus ripen and brown; don't cut them off.

Time to move houseplants outside, but keep a watchful eye for a late frost.

If you want larger peonies, remove the side buds, allowing those on the top of the stem to become bigger and showier.

Stake taller perennials now before they grow too tall.

Repair garden borders.

NOTES

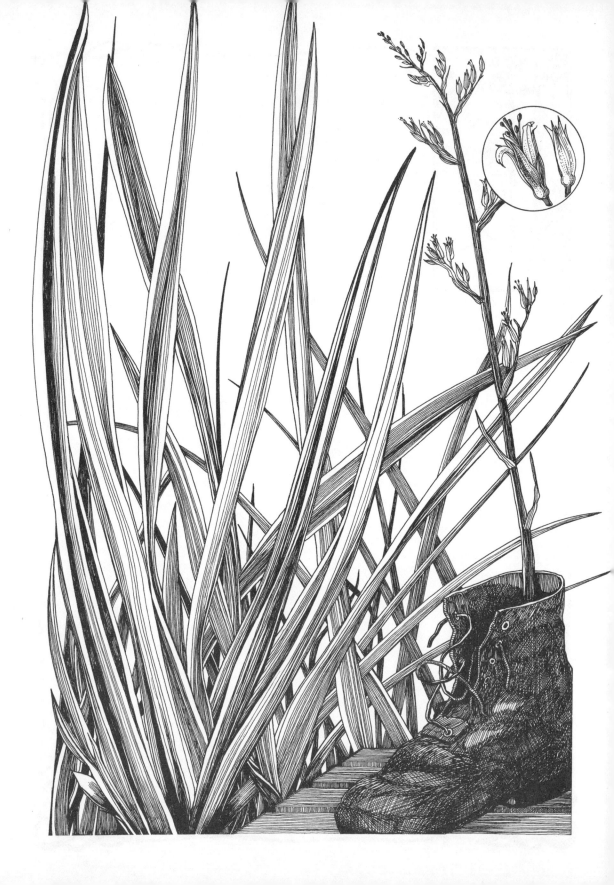

And in mine opinion, I could highly commend your
Orchard, if either through it, or hard by it there should
runne a pleasant River with silver streams: you might sit
in your Mount, and angle a peckled Trout, or fleighty
Eele, or some other dainty Fish. Or moats, whereon you
might row with a Boate, and fishe with Nettes.
   WILLIAM LAWSON

Note that in the above description of an orchard, written in the
year 1618, there are two things necessary for enjoyment: a place to
sit and some water. Moats, silver streams, and pleasant rivers are
beyond the grasp of most gardeners of today, but in any one plot of
land dedicated to plants, there must be a place for a small garden
pool, even if only a plastic liner in a shallow depression, a fiber-
glass tub, or, if you are lucky, half an old oaken barrel. The barrel is
truly a matter of good luck (you live close to a distillery that has
decided to switch to plastic), but most aquatic supply houses now
sell heavy-duty plastic sheets that are used to hold water for a
season (after being placed over a thin layer of sand to prevent
piercing by sharp rocks) and preformed fiber-glass pools. The latter
are placed directly in a dug hole with the edge hidden under a row of
bricks or stones. They come in various shapes including kidney,
round, square, and free-form. With the addition of an electrically
operated waterfall kit, a few goldfish, and some tropical water
lilies, a whole new vista will expand before your eyes.

With the further addition of some solidly built garden furniture,
you can sit with comfort after a hard day's work and watch the
dragonflies dart across your rippled pool.

AN OLD-FASHIONED FLOWER

The carnation, or pink (see p. 55) is mentioned in John Parkin-
son's book *Paradisi in Sole Paradisus Terrestris* forty-nine times,
and that was back in 1629. One hundred years before that first
garden book was published, two carnations are found carefully
rendered in an illuminated manuscript, *The Prayer Book of Charles
the Bold of Burgundy*. Thus, to call this charming flower "old-
fashioned" is a bit of an understatement.

During Elizabethan times, carnations and pinks were in every
garden worth its salt, but by the early 1800s the wealthy gardener
had started to eschew these fragrant treasures, thinking them flowers of the common folk. Flowers, though, like most of the pursuits

NEW ZEALAND FLAX

The plant pictured on the opposite page is a half-hardy evergreen that will do beautifully
in a pot, where the striking
swordlike leaves make a decorative statement both in the home
and on the patio.

A member of the flax family
(fibers from these plants are
used to manufacture rope and
twine), *Phormium tenax* prefers a sandy soil mix under full
sun, with minimum temperatures of 40°–45°F. during the
winter. Plants are very tough
and impervious to pests and
disease. Propagation is by
division of mature clumps in
spring. Keep the soil moist
during the summer months.

Mature plants will flower,
but mine have resisted up to
now. The cut branch in the gardener's boot shows the typical
flowers with a closeup in the
inset.

There are a number of cultivars available on the market,
but many do not come true from
seed.

Carnation
Dianthus × Allwoodii

SUMMER PERENNIALS
The perennials in the drawing are from top right candylilies *(Belamcanda × Pardancanda)*, geums *(Geum Quellyon)*, spiderworts *(Tradescantia × Andersoniana)*, fleabanes *(Erigeron aurantiacus)*, a shasta daisy *(Chrysanthemum × superbum)*, and a columbine *(Aquilegia vulgaris)*.

of man, fall into cycles of fashion, and during the reign of Queen Victoria, the carnation and pink (the first is *Dianthus caryophyllus*, the second *D. plumarius*) rose again in popularity, so much so that in 1897 one new variety sold for $3,000.

These garden flowers are not to be confused with the perpetual-flowering carnation sold by florists; those are tender perennials and only for the greenhouse up north.

In 1902, the nursery firm of Messrs. Allwood crossed the old-fashioned pink with one of the perpetual-flowering varieties and created the Allwood Laced Pink. In 1980, I purchased seeds from England, and one year later, in June, they bloomed. The flowers have that wonderful carnation scent, are brilliant pinks or white, all with a pheasant-eye center, and stand some twelve inches tall.

These flowers are said to resent overly acid soil—a problem that is always at hand in my garden—so I think they owe their health to the fact that where they now grow once stood a cement and stone foundation. They do not need a rich soil, but it should be well drained. Add a dash of bone meal every spring.

Nothing is more completely the child of art than a garden.
Sir Walter Scott

SUMMER PERENNIALS

The six garden perennials on the following page are all fine and delightful additions to any flower border. All are hybrids developed from tough wild plants and require only minimum maintenance in order to brighten your garden outlook every year.

The columbines pictured *(Aquilegia vulgaris)* are the McKana Hybrids, long-spurred blossoms of pink, red, blue, yellow, and cream that last through the end of June—and if spent blossoms are picked, well into summer. Plants may be divided in the fall. You can easily expand a collection by growing plants from commercial seed as columbines germinate with ease. Seeds that you gather in your garden will not produce plants true to type as all columbines interhybridize with each, so quality of flowers will vary greatly.

Columbine leaves are a favorite food of the leaf miner; their larvae will tunnel through, making pale green markings—almost like script writing—on individual leaves, but plants are generally unharmed.

The candylily *(Belamcanda × Pardancanda)* is a new flower developed by crossing the blackberry lily *(Belamcanda chinensis)* with various Asian species. The plants produce iris-shaped, spotted blossoms of purple, yellow, red, orange, and blue. Though individual flowers last only one day, there are many buds on one stem. Plants are pest-free and very hardy.

The fleabanes *(Erigeron)* have produced a number of garden plants with daisylike flowers complete with bright yellow centers. *E. aurantiacus* comes from Turkestan and produces solitary orange

blossoms on nine-inch stems. They make excellent cut flowers. Plants prefer a moist, well-drained situation but are really not too choosy as to position. Cut spent flowers to encourage further bloom. Propagation is by division in the fall or early spring.

The shasta daisy *(Chrysanthemum × superbum)* is a glorious daisy hybrid of the Portuguese daisy *(C. lacustre)* and the daisy chrysanthemum *(C. maximum)* from the Pyrenees. Plants are very hardy and free-flowering. The cultivar "Alaska" is an older variety with three-inch-wide flowers on two- to three-foot stems. They are also excellent for cutting. Propagation is by division, and plants should be lifted and reset every three years to produce maximum-size flowers.

Geums comprise over fifty species of brightly colored and long-lasting flowers. *Geum Quellyon* (listed in most sources as *G. chiloense)* has one hybrid, "Mrs. Bradshaw," that produces double flowers of a brilliant orange-red, three-inches across on two-foot stems. Plants prefer full sun but will grow well in partial shade. Lift and divide every three years.

The spiderworts *(Tradescantia virginiana)* are a wildflower of North America that have, through hydridization, led to a collection of fine garden plants with three-petaled flowers of white, purple, rose, blue, and a number of in-between shades. They like a moist soil and quickly grow into large clumps of spear-shaped leaves that often need staking (see below). I cut the clumps to the ground after flowering is over, and a second crop of leaves and flowers then develop. Hybrids belong to the botanical listing *T. × Andersoniana.*

SUNDROPS IN THE GARDEN

As I look out of my window at the front garden covered with the morning's dew, I see a vast billowy cloud of bright, bright yellow that stretches from the driveway to the fields below: The sundrops *(Oenothera fruticosa)* are in bloom.

These plants are not idly named; the spirits of all the poetic muses stood by the first person who saw these delicate flowers of early summer and dubbed them with a name that inferred that molten drops of the sun had fallen to the earth, there to root and grow.

Sundrops are day-blooming members of the evening primrose family. They bear their bright yellow flowers in clusters on stems that usually grow from one to two feet high. Individual flowers are about two inches across, each having four petals of the golden hue. Some gardeners think them common because they spread with ease, but this trait can be used to your advantage: That bare and dry area on the side of a bank can now be covered with plants and flowers. Being shallow-rooted, unwanted plants are easily pulled out of the ground if you feel that your garden is threatened.

Sundrops will adapt to almost any soil conditions and even tolerate a bit of shade.

Gather in early winter, the seed heads of most of the oenotheras are useful in dried arrangements.

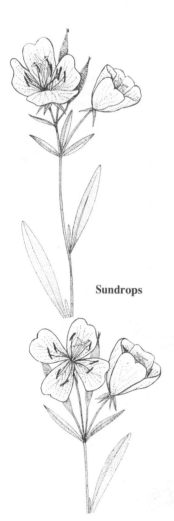

Sundrops

Many garden perennials quickly grow too tall to support themselves and the garden is literally full of flops. There are a number of ways to prevent this from happening, including the placing of twigs and branches about for bracing, various combinations of stakes and twine, or galvanized-wire plant supports made of rings that are used in conjunction with three legs. The last looks the best and can be reused year after year. The only requirement is the placing of the support over the plant early enough to allow stems to grow through the rings. Rings come in three sizes, from twelve through twenty-two inches in diameter, while legs come in three lengths, from eighteen to thirty-six inches.

Support rings

THE SPIRAL RUSH

Rushes belong to a rather small family of plants, the Juncaceae. The name derives from the Latin word *juncere,* or rush, and quite likely refers to the use of rushes in the manufacture of furniture seating.

Most of these plants come from cold and barren lands where their main value is in binding the soil from erosion.

The common rush *(Juncus effusus)* is found in wet and swampy conditions or on occasion in very dry and poor soil. The rootstock is of the creeping variety, the stems are pale green and very pliant, ending in a point. There are no leaves, only a few brown wrappings at the base of the plant. Flowers occur halfway up the stems, forming side panicles of greenish-brown spikelets. When plants are used in groups within a naturalized area, or singly against a stone or brick background, they are most attractive, with stems that persist throughout the winter, often turning rust-red in the fall.

There is one species that comes from Japan, the spiral rush *(J. effusus spiralis),* which produces fifteen- to twenty-inch stems that grow in tight or loose spirals, just like corkscrews. It's a strange and yet charming plant for a moist spot in the garden.

Spiral rush

ANNUALS FOR THE GARDEN

Annuals bloom for only one season, but that short time is generally ablaze with color, for annual plants and flowers give far more in floral effort than is ever extended by the typical gardener. Annuals will grow in almost any soil except hardpan and rock. You need only water them, remove dead blossoms to extend the blooming period, and start seed germination early indoors so they are ready to bloom when spring and summer roll around.

The illustration shows five colorful and rather uncommon annuals suited for both the flower garden and the cutting garden.

Clockwise from top right: A veteran flower from the gardens of the Victorian period is Flora's-paintbrush *(Emilia javanica,* or, in some seed catalogs, *Cacalia coccinea)* with its red-orange blossoms that freely bloom for most of the summer season; Love-in-a-mist *(Nigella damascena)* produces feathery white, pink, or pastel-blue flowers in combination with very finely cut foliage — and interesting seedpods, too; the garden nasturtium *(Tropaeolum majus),* famous for its colorful and sweet-smelling flowers and for its leaves, which give a peppery taste to fresh salads; Tickseed *(Coreopsis tinctoria)* has bright yellow daisy-type flowers with center rings of glowing brownish-orange; and Corn cockle *(Agrostemma githago* **'Milas'**), a particular cultivar that produces larger flowers than the typical plant and of a deeper shade of lavender-pink.

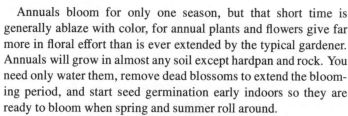

A VASE OF ANNUALS
The flowers in the vase at right are described in the text.

Remember that there are two types of annuals listed in nursery catalogs:

H.A.—meaning hardy annual; plants that will tolerate frosts to a greater or lesser degree according to their type, many being able to survive a winter outside in North America where they will germinate the following spring.

H.H.A.—half-hardy annual; plants that probably won't survive frosts. They are usually started indoors, using a bottom heat of 60°F. to ensure germination, and need to be "hardened off" for about a week before being transplanted outdoors when frost danger is past. Either place them in a cold frame or put them in a protected place to be brought inside again if low temperatures threaten. Most seed packets of today give full instructions on the back, especially if anything unusual is demanded.

MINT FOR FLAVORING

During the warm days of the year, there is no finer herb to have in good supply than mint, either spearmint *(Mentha spicata)* or peppermint *(M. piperita).* They are both hardy perennials and once started in your garden must be watched since both ramble all over with underground runners. In fact, it's best to contain them in one area of damp soil by using metal edging of the type sold to separate the lawn from the garden. The taste of fresh mint is worth the effort of keeping the plants contained. Give them partial shade. Both plants grow to a height of some twenty inches.

Mint

Mint is of course traditional with lamb, and the leaves are fine in salads, many cooked vegetables, and soups. Spearmint is the traditional flavoring for mint juleps and is excellent when added to iced tea.

THE SEA ONION

Some years ago, as a gift from a houseplant aficionado, I received a green ball, four inches in diameter, with a slight depression that marked the top and a few dried roots that signified the bottom. The accompanying letter called the green aggie a "climbing sea onion" or *Bowiea volubilis.* "Plant it in a five-inch pot," the letter said, "with a soil mix of one-third good potting soil, one-third composted manure, and one-third sharp sand for good drainage, placing the top half of the bulb above the soil line. Water if after growth begins and let the soil dry out between waterings. Growth will die back in late spring or fall depending on when you have started the plant. Keep temperatures above 50°F."

I did as directed and was soon rewarded by twining stems, tiny green flowers, and minuscule leaves represented by tiny triangular flaps of green where branchlet grows from branch. In order to give the rampant vine a holdfast, I put its pot inside a Japanese basket (shown in the drawing). When the foliage starts to yellow and dry, I withhold water and give the bulb a rest for a few months.

Propagation is by seed or offsets. A healthy bulb should eventually reach a diameter of eight to nine inches, with a corresponding increase in stem production.

The sea onion will always elicit comments by visiting gardeners.

A BOG GARDEN

The hot days of July and the dog days of August will soon be upon us and the major part of our flower garden will have gone through its yearly paces, so thoughts might turn now to a couple of projects.

One such project could be the establishment of a bog garden, allowing you to grow the many plants that will not thrive in the harsh and dry environment of the garden border. The North American pitcher plant *(Sarracenia purpurea),* a number of native and foreign orchids, and all manner of interesting grasses and sedges will put on an annual show and, because of constant water, do well even in dry years.

Find a spot of ground as large as you feel will remain under your control; if it's near a downspout from your roof, all the better. Remove all the soil from an arbitrarily selected irregular shape to a depth of two to three feet, leaving the hole with slightly sloping sides. Make sure these sides are free of sharp rocks, and then proceed to line the cavity with either heavy wet clay or black plastic, depending on the amount of work you're willing to do and whether you're a purist or not.

Replace the soil that you've removed with a mix of peat moss and good garden loam or humus, using one-half of each. If the soil that

THE SEA ONION

The plant twining about a basket in the drawing at right is a mature sea onion.

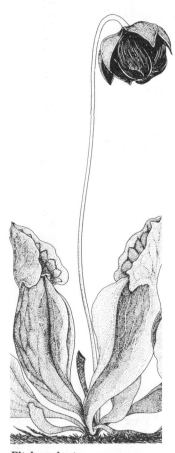

Pitcher plant

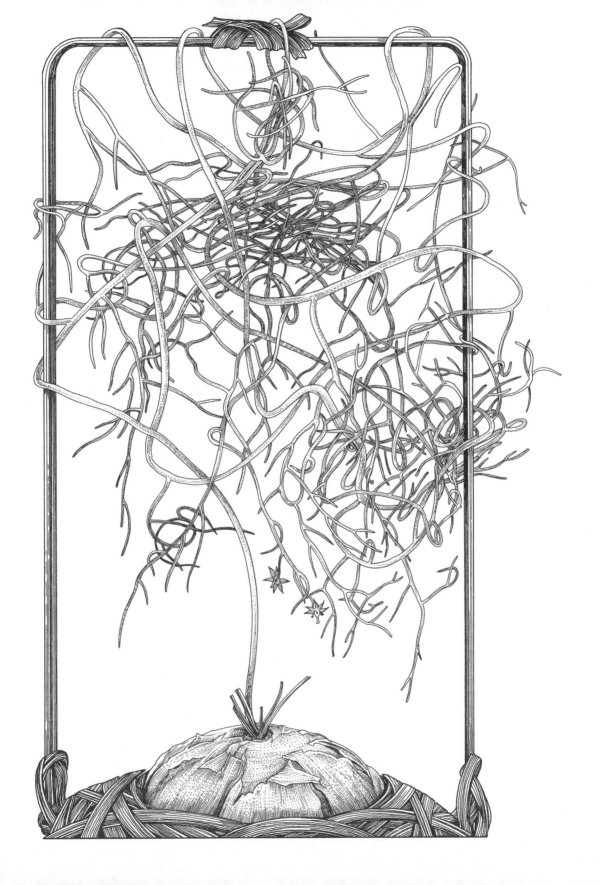

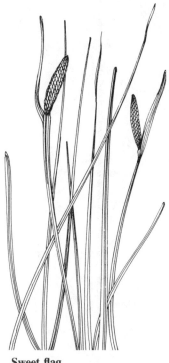

Sweet flag

was removed was of good quality, use that. When the hole is full, start to wet the mix with a garden hose. Don't use water full force, but let it flow in, as the peat moss will take quite a while to become saturated. It's helpful to include a plastic container of about a gallon with no bottom openings and a wide top, about a foot under the surface to act as a water trap for the deeper-rooted bog plants.

Even old sinks can be used to create these gardens, carefully covering the white edges with rocks or stones.

Among the plants that will do well in bog surroundings are sweet flag *(Acorus calamus)*, any number of wild water irises, cardinal flower *(Lobelia cardinalis)*, and the marsh marigold *(Caltha palustris)*. See the list of suggested reading for more books on water and bog gardening.

HINTS FOR JUNE

Make sure your hanging plants are watered every day before they die of thirst.

Start next year's perennials and biennials from seed.

Don't forget to dead-head annuals to keep up the bloom.

Watch for the Japanese-beetle invasion.

Remove the spent flowers from rhododendrons and lilacs.

Don't forget to water any transplants in hot weather.

Remember to fix up the greenhouse; now is the time to prepare for next winter.

Have a garden party.

Stake delphiniums if you haven't already.

Check the nurseries for season-end sales.

Order bulbs for fall.

Plan a day lily bed of early, middle, and late bloomers for flowers all year long.

Notes

A stone hewn into a gracefully ornamented vase or urn has a value which it did not before possess; a yew hedge clipped into a fortification is only defaced. The one is a product of art, the other a distortion of nature.

SIR WALTER SCOTT

I love the topiary art, with its trimness and primness, and its open avowal of its artificial character. It repudiates at the first glance the skulking and cowardly *"celare artem"* principle, and, in its vegetable sculpture, is the properest transition from the architecture of the house to the natural beauties of the grove and paddock.

T. JAMES

One of the wonderful things about gardening is that there is no one way about it. Everything is entirely up to you, the gardener; what you say goes! Sir Walter thought artifice in the garden a loathsome thing, while Mr. James exclaims that the business of pretending to be natural, of hiding art behind the cloak of nature, is a terrible principle. Let's assume both to be correct and go outside to weed....

A FEW NOTES ON HEAT

Of course there is no need to dwell on the heat of July; it is always hot—much too hot! And when that sun beats down in combination with a brisk wind, potted plants dry out with undue speed; before you turn around, your fuchsia is drooping too far for its own good, or the verbena is done to a turn.

So take additional time to check your plants that are summering out-of-doors and make sure they have enough water to last through the hot hours of the day. Take additional care with any cuttings or transplants in peat pots as the pot fibers act as wicks, evaporating valuable soil water to the air. One watering trick is to put ice cubes on top of soil in hanging pots. The cold will not hurt the plants, and the slow melt will provide water all day long.

On the other end of the scale, don't let your plants sit in saucers full of water and waterlog the soil.

Remember to acclimate houseplants to the outdoors and the summer sun by exposing them in stages. Light shade will do for the first day; bring them into the open more on each successive day. Leaves can burn as easily as skin.

LILY-OF-THE-NILE

The Egyptian lily *(Agapanthus africanus)*, or lily-of-the-Nile, is a member of the family Amaryllidaceae. It does well outside in warm regions or resides in a tub year-round up north. The plants thrive in any fertile and well-drained soil, with full sun in the summer and monthly applications of plant food from April to September. Water them well while in active growth and you will be rewarded with large heads of flowers in bloom for a month or more. They are excellent as cut flowers, and the dried seed heads are a fine addition to winter bouquets.

From October through May (depending on your location), move them indoors to a frost-free spot, giving only enough water to keep soil moist. Remove any leaves that turn yellow as they will rot.

Propagate by division. Seeds will germinate, but it will take up to three years for a flowering plant to develop.

The drawing shows the white form known as *A. orientalis* 'Albidus'.

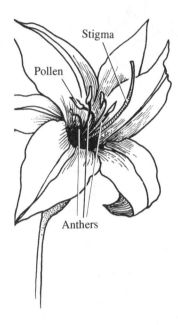

Stigma

Pollen

Anthers

BREEDING YOUR OWN DAY LILIES

Day lilies, with their large flowers, are fine subjects for interbreeding experiments. You can transfer the pollen (the yellow powder that contains the male sex cells) from one blossom to the female stigma (the flattened top of the long rod that stands above the six anthers), thus starting the process of setting seed.

Start early in the morning and use a cotton swab, but first remove the six anthers from the flower of your choice to prevent an accidental cross. After pollenizing, cover the blossom with a small paper or plastic bag and maintain careful records. The next day remove the bag and watch the pod as it swells and matures. When fully ripe and ready to split, remove the shiny black seeds within.

Seeds may be germinated in a cool spot (40°–60°F.) indoors or planted outside in the fall to germinate the following spring.

THE TAWNY DAY LILY

The scientific name of the wild day lily is *Hemerocallis fulva* — *hemero* being Greek for beautiful and *callis* Greek for day (each individual blossom opens, matures, and withers in twenty-four hours) and *fulva* the Latin word for tawny or an orange-tan color.

They were first described in a garden text published in 1629: growers in boggy spots of Germany, only having reached England in 1575. Originally they were brought over the trade routes from China.

When settlers came to America from England and Europe, they brought some of their favorite flowers to brighten the colonial garden. But as a homesteader's time was at a premium, any plant that did make the trip had to be hardy and able to withstand a good deal of neglect—in essence, a beautiful weed.

Thus the common day lilies that line the rural roadsides of North America are all escapees of early gardens. Impervious to the black macadam that stops a few short inches from their roots, and unaffected by the residues of chemicals used to melt winter ice a few short months before, they first begin to bloom about the first of July when the summer sun is hottest.

Day lilies are virtually carefree. They require no special attentions — although like most living things, the more care you do provide, the better they will grow. These plants will hold dry, rocky banks together or grow with perfect ease in moist soil by the water's edge.

Late in the 1800s, plant breeders saw the potential in the common day lily and began to develop new varieties or cultivars using the pollen of the tawny, the lemon lily (a close relative), and other species from Japan and Europe. When research was slowed in Europe as a result of the two world wars, America took up the day-lily banner and from a humble beginning it is estimated that there are well over 12,000 varieties and more on the way.

They prefer full sun in the North, partial shade in the Deep South. Propagation is by division for the wild day lily (*H. fulva* does not set seed) and by division or seed for the domesticated types. Plants may be left in one spot for many years, but once blooming starts to decline, it's time to divide.

By carefully selecting day-lily varieties, you can have bloom in your garden from early spring through the heat of summer and on into fall. There are dwarf types for the rock garden, a few varieties that will bloom twice in one growing season, and all the colors in the rainbow except white and blue.

COOKING WITH THE DAY LILY

In addition to all its superior garden qualities, the day lily is also used as food. The Chinese have used its flowers in cooking for centuries and today Chinese recipes call for dried lily flowers—*gum jum* — found in Chinese groceries under such English names as "golden needles" or "tiger flowers."

Use your own blossoms by picking them early in the morning as they just begin to open. Remove the six stamens (they hold the yellow pollen) and the long central pistil. All you use are the petals.

Day Lily Chicken
1 whole chicken breast, skinned,
   boned, and sliced thin
1 small onion, chopped
1 tablespoon soy sauce
1 tablespoon cornstarch
1 teaspoon chopped fresh ginger
3 tablespoons oil, divided
1 small onion, sliced
3 cups fresh day-lily petals
¼ cup water

In a bowl, mix the chicken, chopped onion, soy sauce, ginger, and cornstarch. In a wok or skillet, heat two tablespoons of the oil until very hot but not smoking; add the chicken mixture and stir-fry for two minutes. Remove from the heat and set aside. Wipe out the pan and brown the sliced onions in the remaining oil. Add lily petals, water, and the chicken mixture. Cook and stir for two minutes or until the sauce has thickened. Makes two or three servings depending on your appetite.

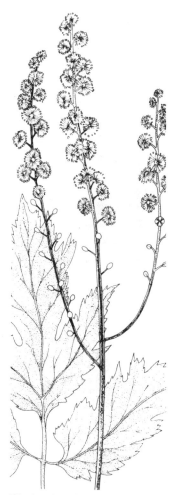

Black cohosh

AT THE BOG'S EDGE

Many of our favorite wildflowers will forever resent being planted in a typical garden setting, but will do beautifully when planted on the edge of a bog or pool.

Last year I started a black cohosh or snakeroot *(Cimicifuga racemosa),* so called because the flowers have a rather rank odor, supposedly used by the American Indians as a primitive type of 6-12. Its powers as an insect repellent are limited, but as a garden perennial there are few finer plants. When placed at the bog's edge, the plants soon grew to a height of nine feet, and the flowers on their long slender wands rose three feet above that.

Another American flower that does well at water's edge is the moccasin flower *(Cypripedium acaule),* the wild orchid, which requires a moist and acid soil. The roots live in conjunction with a soil fungus, so rather than dig them up from the wild, order them from a commercial source.

Sweet flag *(Acorus calamus)* was once grown commercially as the source of a drug, calamus. It imparts a sweet smell to all parts of the plant and when crushed in the fingers has a pungent, bitter taste. It has been used since the days of early Greece for diseases of the eye, and supposedly sailors would chew the root to relieve flatulence and toothache, a deadly combination. It's also been used in hair tonics. Sweet flag likes full sun.

The annual grasses are rarely grown for their foliage but for the flowers and seeds — for decoration in the garden, fresh-cut bouquets, and dried arrangements for winter.

As a general rule, the annuals require a spot in full summer sun, but they are not fussy as to soil conditions. In order to have a sequence of bloom throughout the season, start some plants indoors in early spring. Outdoors in the garden, plants should be six inches to one foot apart, depending on their final height.

The grasses on the preceding page are some of the more decorative annuals and perennials available.

(1) Hare's-tail grass *(Lagurus ovatus)* is a hardy annual that produces a great many terminal spikes that look exactly like their namesakes. Eighteen to twenty-four inches in height, the flower heads are easily dried and will not shatter with age.

(2) Job's tears *(Coix lacryma-jobi),* a close relative of corn, has the distinction of being one of the oldest ornamental grasses in cultivation, harking back to the fourteenth century. The seeds fall readily from the plant at maturity and are hard, white, streaked with gray or black, and very shiny. They have been used for years in the making of jewelry, especially rosaries. The plants like some shade, a damper soil than the rest, and are frost-tender. At maturity, leaves are up to four feet tall.

Bromegrass *(Bromus madritensis)* is a hardy annual, growing to a height of about two feet and featuring very attractive flowers and seeds that retain their character when dried.

Quaking grass *(Briza maxima)* is a half-hardy annual, native to southern Europe where it's been in cultivation as a garden ornament for over 200 years. The spikelets quiver and quake with every gentle breeze. It grows to three feet and is rather ungainly-looking so is best cultivated for the flowers when picked.

The perennial grasses can be either grown from seed or purchased as mature plants from nurseries. They all require a fertile, well-drained soil, generally in full sun. The only chore connected with the perennials is pruning the dead stems and leaves in the early spring and dividing mature clumps of some of the larger varieties. All are hardy in zone 5.

(3) Bulbous oat grass *(Arrhenatherum elatius* var. *bulbosum* **'Variegatum')** produces a white-and-green variegated leaf eight to eighteen inches tall, that grows from a bulblike bottom that is really swollen nodes on the stem. Each "bulb" will produce a plant when divided. In cold climates, the leaves retain their shape and color well into December.

(4) Northern sea oats *(Chasmanthium latifolium* — still called *Uniola latifolia* in many catalogs) is the only grass that will survive in summer shade. The plant is attractive and the flowers make it unique. After the first frost, leaves and flowers turn a rich tannish-brown and remain on the plant well into early winter.

ORNAMENTAL GRASSES

The grasses in the drawing at left are identified with the text in the key below:

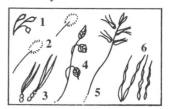

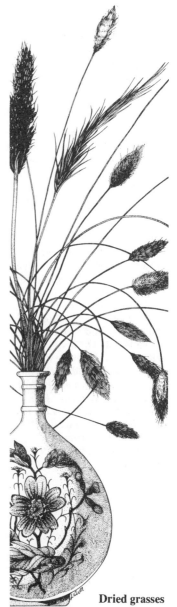

Dried grasses

(5) Bottlebrush grass *(Hystrix patula)* is a most attractive grass of the northeastern woodlands and closely resembles its namesake. It grows from three to four feet tall and the awned spikelets look well in dried arrangements.

(6) Striped orchard grass *(Dactylis glomerata* **'Variegata')** grows up to two feet tall. This variegated form of a common forage grass for cattle has one of the finest greens in the garden, almost the color of limes. The flowers are fine for a wild bouquet, but the grace is in the plant.

ON DRYING GRASSES

If you wish to use grasses (or other plants) for dried bouquets, the only equipment you will need is wire coat hangers, paper twist ties left over from plastic bags, and a sharp knife or scissors.

Gather the grasses in midafternoon on a dry and sunny day, after the dews of morning have evaporated and before the afternoon damp sets in. Pick stems with blossoms that are not yet completely open, and cut the stems as long as you can; it's much easier to trim stems for a shorter arrangement than to glue stems back together for length. Strip any excess leaves from the stem — these will only shrivel into unattractiveness during the drying process—but leave the seed heads. Tie small bunches of stems together loosely, enabling air to pass easily between stems, and hang them upside down on wire coat hangers, again allowing plenty of room between bunches. Hang the hangers well apart in a basement room or garage that is cool, dry, dark, and airy. The cool temperature prevents the plant sap from drying too quickly and forcing the spikelets to go to seed; the dry and airy atmosphere prevents the formation of mold and mildew; and the darkness prevents premature fading of the floral parts.

Check your bundles every few days; since the stems shrink as they dry, many could fall to the floor and be ruined.

A very light misting with hairspray is often helpful in holding very delicate seed heads together.

WAYS TO WATER

The illustration on the following page shows fourteen different appliances to help the gardener with the chores of watering, and this does not take hoses into account. Hoses, by the by, come in five-eighth-inch diameter, half-inch diameter, and three-quarter-inch diameter, and are made of plastic, vinyl, and vinyl and rubber. The last is the most expensive and, of course, gives you the most for the money. Always keep a few hose washers on hand along with at least two clinching members of your hose size for repairing leaks.

(1) Soil-soaker hoses are made of canvas duck that allows water to gently leak through the pores, soaking the ground that it passes over. (2) Fogg-it is a hose nozzle that produces a fine foglike spray. (3) The water breaker turns any high-pressure stream of water into a gentle flow. (4) Flaring rose produces a wide and soft spray for seedlings. (5) The fertilizer applicator can be used with any water-

VARIEGATED PLANTS

One of the more interesting approaches to gardening is building a plant collection around a theme. Vita Sackville-West designed an all-white garden at Sissinghurst in England that became the talk of the garden world; E.A. Bowles set aside one section of his garden for strange and twisted plants; other gardeners grow rhododendron collections or deal exclusively with roses; still others plant only wildflowers.

A most interesting garden can be designed using only variegated plants—leaves that evidence two or more colors, often in blotches and usually green and white, though yellow, various greens, and even reds are often found. The drawing at right shows clockwise from top right: *Hosta undulata* 'Mediopicta'; *Hydrangea macrophylla* 'Variegated Mariesii'; *Pieris japonica* 'Variegata'; *Lamium maculatum* 'Beacon Silver'; *Pachysandra terminalis* 'Variegata'; and *Actinidia Kolomikta*.

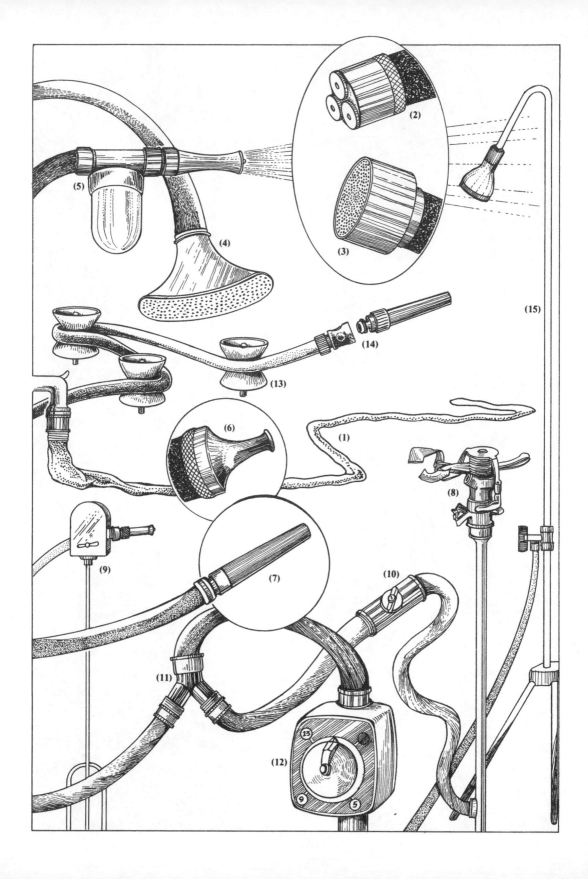

ing or sprinkling device; it holds fertilizer cartridges for a timed release. (6) The sweeper nozzle generates a powerful stream of water for hosing down patios, sidewalks, driveways, etc. (7) Water miser shuts itself off when dropped. (8) The rainbird sprinkler sends an endless variety of sprays over a large garden plot. (9) The rainspike will hold your garden hose and nozzle in a number of watering positions. (10) The hose shutoff enables you to turn off water at any place on the hose. (11) The Y connection gives you two hoses for one. (12) The water timer makes any sprinkler automatic by metering any amount of water up to 1,400 gallons for five minutes to four hours. (13) Spin Guides will guide the hose from rampaging through the garden bed. (14) The Gardena system is made of high-impact plastic and enables the gardener to instantly lock into the hose any number of nozzles, extensions, and even a brush to wash the car. (15) The Portable Shower brings water to the overheated gardener or the active child.

WAYS TO WATER
The drawing at left shows many of the methods to move water about the garden.

A BEAUTIFUL TERRESTRIAL ORCHID

Disa uniflora is a terrestrial orchid with blossoms of varying shades of orange and red. It's an orchid that grows in peaty soils at the edges of bogs or streams where the atmosphere is damp and cool. These qualities make it a wonderful addition to the orchid fancier's collection, especially when providing heat is a difficulty.

The plants do very well in the same environment as cymbidiums. They like bright light and sun only if temperatures are low: below 90°F. in summer and above 32°F. in winter; freezing will kill the plants. The best temperatures during the winter are 40°–60°F.

Disas are never completely dormant and grow slowly throughout the seasons. Before and after flowering, new shoots are produced that will flower the following year. A dilute fertilizer should be given during active growth, and watering itself should continue throughout the year so the potting mix is kept moist at all times.

Mixes may consist of peat, sand, perlite, screened sphagnum moss, and vermiculite in varying amounts.

Mature plants flower during June and July. If buds appear on a plant that has not produced additional offsets for the following year, remove the buds or enjoy the flower and usually lose the plant.

Repot after flowering, with soil removed and old roots, stems, and leaf rosettes thrown out while potting the fresh growth for the following season.

HINTS FOR JULY

Help others in the vegetable garden.

Order more bulbs for fall. Try some species tulips in the rock garden.

Cut back spent delphiniums to encourage a second crop of flowers.

Keep dead-heading annuals for continued bloom.

Don't cut the lawn too closely—or, better yet, put in a flagstone path and do away with the lawn entirely.

AN AFRICAN ORCHID
The drawing on the next page shows a disa orchid in full bloom with three more buds lined up in the wings.

NOTES

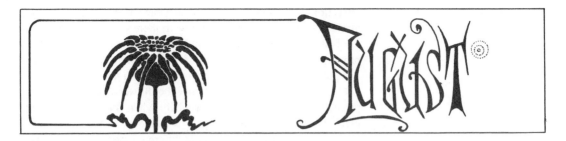

And now to sum up as to a garden. Large or small, it should look both orderly and rich. It should be well fenced from the outside world. It should by no means imitate either the wilfulness or the wildness of Nature, but should look like a thing never to be seen except near a house. It should, in fact, look like a part of the house.

WILLIAM MORRIS

Till you grow your own potatoes, you do not really begin to live. A house without a garden is a temporary home.

R. LeGALLIENNE

August is a fine month to take stock of the garden: The blaze of early summer bloom is past—even the potent annuals have started to slow their flowering—yet it's too early to divide and transplant for the fall or set out bulbs for next year. Pick up paper and pen, making notes of what plants to move next spring or any special items slated for next season that require advance preparation: Building a reflecting pool? Another perennial border? Perhaps a small garden of dwarf conifers? For as William Morris said, the garden is the extension of the home.

MINIATURE ROSES

Miniature roses have the same cultural requirements as their larger relatives, with one exception: It's not easy to dig up a hybrid tea rose and bring it indoors for the winter, but with the miniatures there's no problem at all.

Outside, these roses need good garden soil, good drainage, and at least eight hours of sun every day. Fertilizer for roses should be added two or three times a year during the growing season.

When winter comes, either mound soil over the frozen earth and the dormant miniatures (they are hardier than their bigger cousins, but no sense taking chances in zone 5 or below) or, after dormancy has arrived, dig up a few, put them in four-inch pots, place in a south window with at least six hours of light—or artificial lights—and watch them go. Then when spring comes around, plant them outside once more in the regular garden.

THE BONNET BELLFLOWER

This particular plant might not be everyone's cup of tea. The plant itself is not very interesting: slight green stems, a few small leaves, erect for a while but soon beginning to sprawl. What's the

MINIATURE ROSES

Miniature roses are all descended from one flower, *Rosa chinensis* 'Minima'. The flowers pictured at left and reading from the left are the ten-inch-tall 'September Days' of bright yellow, 'Cupcake' of bright pink blooms, and the highly fragrant lavender 'Angel Darling'. I apologize for the names —they are the choice of the nursery.

Russian buffalo grass

Red peppers

THE BEAUTIFUL BELL
   The blooming *Codonopsis clematidea* has been drawn to show the intricate and delicate shading on the inside of the bell. Be sure to provide winter protection where weather is severe.

attraction? The flower. It's a nodding bell of the palest of blues; almost, but not quite, white. But wait, there's more. The inside of the bell is marked with two bands of purple, bright yellow, dark brown, and pale bands or veins of blue. Flowers should be picked and put in water to really enjoy their particular beauty.

Codonopsis are called the "bonnet bellflowers." They need some protection north of zone 6, especially when there is no winter's blanket of snow, so mulching is a good idea. They germinate readily from seed, and a number of different varieties are offered by many of the plant societies. Soil should have good drainage and be slightly on the acid side.

The foliage has a slight foxy smell when bruised but not enough to be offensive.

THE FIRE OF THE PEPPER, THE SWEET SMELL OF THE MEADOW

There are two wonderful ways to remember the joy of the garden when winter winds blow and the sky is dismal and dark. Both are infusions of vodka: one mixed with Russian buffalo grass and the other with red-hot peppers.

Zubrovka

Russian buffalo grass is another species (or it possibly could be the same) of our own American sweet grass or holy grass *(Anthoxanthum odoratum)* often used by the American Indians for flavoring and as a weaving material for baskets and mats. Both species contain a chemical called "coumarin," which imparts a sweet aromatic principle to the plants (it's also found in sweet clover). The Russian variety is described in *Flora of the U.S.S.R.* as a favorite food of bison in the Belovezha Thicket, hence the common name.

Neither of the grasses mentioned is particularly attractive for the formal garden, so why bother to grow them? The Russian grass is used to change ordinary vodka to zubrovka by merely adding three or four blades to a quart of spirits. In a few weeks the sweet odor is imparted to the vodka and opening up a tainted bottle is to smell the meadow in the height of summer. The longer it sits, the better it gets and the vodka a just so slight hint of green. Use only inexpensive vodka for zubrovka and for the "hot vodka" below.

Hot Vodka

Hot vodka is exactly what the name implies: The first sip is a fiery shock to the tongue and palate, then it mellows until the next sip starts the round again; meanwhile, the appetite for dinner is increased fourfold. For friends who are not inclined to hot food or drink, cut the original liqueur with pure vodka, or leave it alone.

If hot vodka is mixed with cream and cheese to coat fresh pasta, it is a dish of pure marvel.

For each bottle of regular vodka, add three whole, small dried hot peppers and let it sit for about three weeks before tasting. Like

Rudbeckia

Milk thistle

CALIFORNIA GOLD

The flowers of *Eschscholtzia* are among the loveliest to grace a garden. The drawing shows the silken quality of the petals and the torus at the blossom's base.

zubrovka, the longer it sits, the mellower it becomes, but always a mellow heat. As the peppers fade, you can remove them from the bottle, but I leave them in for decorative purposes.

RUDBECKIAS

August would seem an excellent month to pay homage to one of the leading flower families of the garden, the Compositae.

Whether the black-eyed Susan *(Rudbeckia hirta)*, a glowing yellow daisy that hitchhiked in from the West to take up residence in dry fields and along country roadsides; or the orange coneflower *(R. fulgida)*, a reverse carpetbagger that journeyed up from the South; or the biggest of them all, the Texas coneflower *(R. bicolor)*, these flowers are all workhorses of the perennial border.

Originally classified by the father of modern botanical nomenclature, Linnaeus, this genus is named after Olaf Rudbeck (1660-1740) and his son, both professors of botany at Upsala University.

Plant breeders have worked their wonders on *rudbeckias* and we now have garden hybrids with flowers twice as large as nature's first attempts. They begin to bloom in late July and will continue until cut down by frost. All are perennials except the black-eyed Susan, and this demure member of the group will self-seed with such vigor that it can, on occasion, become almost a weed.

Rudbeckias have an amazing resistance to drought, and even badly wilted plants will quickly perk up with a minimum of water. Thus they are most valuable plants when summers are dry. Any soil is acceptable, but they will bloom with more exuberance when given a bit of manure or plant food. It's best to move them in spring, but with enough water it's safe to do it this month.

It's easy to grow these daisies from seed and they will flower the first year. Many new types are now available on the market, including the new "Irish Eyes" that boasts a green center instead of the typical brown.

OUR-LADY'S-THISTLE

Known as milk thistle *(Silybum marianum),* this plant is grown for its foliage; the flowers, except for a few to bear extra seed, should be removed as they are not very attractive. The leaves are cut, spiny, and a beautiful combination of green and speckled white. Sow seeds where the plants are to grow; they do not move well. And although it's listed as a biennial, treat it as an annual since in most of the U.S. it's winter-killed.

Years ago it was grown as a potherb with the roots eaten cooked.

THE CALIFORNIA POPPY

In the late sixteenth century, Spanish sailors journeying along the coast of California looked upon the hillsides awash with a golden hue and named the country "Tierra del Fuego"; others seeing the glowing shores would shout: "Gold! Gold!" and believe for a moment that they had found the true land of *El Dorado;* and one

Father Junipero Serra would spy the golden splendor and shout, "At last I have found the Holy Grail!"

They had all seen the blooms of the California poppy *(Eschscholtzia californica),* a flower as close to the color of burnished gold as you're liable to find in the vegetable kingdom.

The first person to collect and return specimens to England (the then collecting center of the world) was Archibald Menziwa, a naval surgeon and botanist who sailed on a voyage of discovery in 1791 that ended up on the shores of California, but the plants never survived the trip back and the collected seeds never grew.

Then in 1815, Adelbert von Chamisso (a poet whose work Schumann set to music in the song cycle *Frauenliebe und - leben)* went with a Russian scientific expedition to search for the northern passage between the Atlantic and Pacific and was joined on the trip by a young Russian naturalist of German extraction, one Johann Friedrich Eschscholtz.

They never found the shortcut, but von Chamisso rediscovered the poppy and honored Johann with the genus.

In 1890 it became the state flower, and many think it was partly responsible for the poppy boom all over the civilized world: In art, cooking, and culture, the flower was used for everything from butter-pat designs to architectural trim. (The other reason was the romantic attachment to drugs enjoyed by the French and English romantic poets and artists at the century's turn.)

The blossoms, which last three or four days, close at night. They come in the common gold and additional shades of scarlet, terracotta, and white, in single and double blooms (doubles are sterile). The disk at the base of the flower is called a "torus."

Although it's a biennial in California, elsewhere this flower is treated as an annual. Plants thrive in window boxes, planters, and pots, needing only well-drained soil and as much sun as you can provide.

California poppies will continue to bloom well into fall and only stop when cut down by a killing frost.

Collected seed from hybrids will not grow true but will revert to type.

LOOSESTRIFE AND CATTAILS

While driving along the highways and byways of the Northeast in mid- to late August, you might have noticed a purple haze spreading over the low marshes and meadows along the way — a color so intense that all other hues fade by comparison.

The flower belongs to the purple loosestrife *(Lythrum salicaria),* a plant that reached our shores when the Europeans came and has year by year extended its range ever westward.

It's a popular flower in England, and when Shakespeare wrote of Ophelia, "With fantastic garlands did she come, Of crow-flowers, nettles, daisies, and long purples ..." the "long purples" were the loosestrife.

But there is a problem with this plant: Although it brightens up the swamp, it is invasive beyond belief and quickly smothers out the cattail *(Typha angustifolia),* one of the most valuable plants for wildlife.

The part of the plant called the "cattail" is in reality the flower: The upper section is a slender spike of silver-gray staminate flowers (male) that bloom in early summer; the lower and thicker portion is made up of the pistillate (female) flowers.

The uses of cattails are many: Flour can be made from the pollen; the stems and leaves are excellent for thatching; the roots have been used to treat dysentery; the tails when broken up make marvelous stuffing for pillows; young flower spikes make a more than passable cooked vegetable; the pollen may be mixed with other flours to impart color and flavor (better than artificial dyes, too); the sprouts at the end of the rootstock can be used for a vegetable when cooked; the thickened rootstock may be roasted or boiled for food in the wild; the white and tender parts of spring shoots make excellent asparagus; and the pollen has occasionally been utilized by fireworks manufacturers, as it's flammable.

With wildlife, the food and homemaking uses are shared with man: The water birds alone would mourn its loss, as cattails are a fine source of soft lining for nests; and the muskrat, who would lose a favorite comestible.

When you were young and fancy-free, which blossom would you have preferred for thwacking a playmate's head?

Cattail

MORE ON CONTAINER GARDENING

One of the charms of the smaller evergreen conifers is the comparative ease with which they can be grown in containers. For those gardeners in the city with naught but a terrace, or in the suburbs with a small lot, container gardening is a most satisfying pastime.

A container by definition can vary from a small pot or a sunken soapstone sink to a large raised bed in the backyard (see pp. 65 and 66). They all have one thing in common: The soil they contain will be mixed to your specifications and is much easier to readjust than changing a garden or digging up a lot.

The decorative possibilities of such gardens are almost endless. I have an especially fine dwarf redwood *(Sequoia sempervirens* **'Adpressa'***)* that is much too tender to withstand our rugged winters. By planting it in a terra-cotta pot, it becomes an attractive addition to my rock-garden wall in the summer and at Christmastime it comes indoors to be decorated as a living holiday tree.

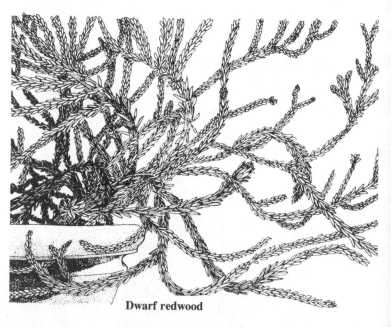

Dwarf redwood

There is one requirement: Plants in small containers will do best if sunk in the ground for the winter and allowed to endure the cold with the rest of the outdoors. If brought indoors, they must have three months of an average temperature of 40°F. Without meeting this condition, the plants will eventually die, for they must have a sustained period of dormancy once a year.

If a potted plant is left outside without being buried or given other protection, the bitter winds striking the pots will soon kill the roots. And if the winds don't do the job, the continual freezing and unfreezing will do it. In the colder parts of the country, there is the additional problem of clay pots that break when the water in their pores freezes and expands.

When you bring small evergreens indoors and provide them with the 40°F., there is one more duty the gardener has. Since the soil around the plant's roots is not frozen solid, the roots continue to draw small amounts of water; they do not stop activities completely. The container must thus be watered every three or four weeks. The soil must not become bone-dry. Never overlook this duty. Evergreens do not evidence wilt as quickly as other plants; by the time the damage is visible, it's usually too late to cure.

After two weeks in the living room for Christmas, the dwarf sequoia goes back to the enclosed sun porch for 40°F. nights and 60°F. days.

Evergreens for Pot Culture

The following slow-growing or naturally dwarf members of the conifer family are excellent for the pot when left in the alpine house or the unheated sun porch. Bring them indoors for a few weeks at a time and let them spend the rest of the winter with good light, water when dry, and that magic temperature of 40°F.

Use a six-inch pot that will accommodate an eight- to ten-inch-high tree. Repot every other year in early fall with a mix of one-third good garden loam, one-third peat moss, and one-third crushed gravel.

Abies balsamea **'Hudsonia'**—the dwarf balsam fir
Chamaecyparis pisifera **'Aurea Compacta Nana'**
C. pisifera **'Squarrosa Minima'**
Juniperus procumbens **'Nana'**
Picea Abies **'Pygmaea'**
Picea glauca **'Echiniformis'**
Pinus Strobus **'Nana'**
Sequoia sempervirens **'Adpressa'**

HINTS FOR AUGUST

Oriental poppies are now dormant and can be moved.

Toward month's end, take cuttings of bedding annuals for inside bloom.

Don't forget those orchids that you hung beneath a tree branch.

Fertilize your hanging plants so they'll continue to bloom into the fall.

Make sure your evergreens are getting enough water to prepare for fall and winter.

Pick a spot for the hole needed for this year's live Christmas tree (see p. 143).

Clean up the greenhouse and get ready for the big move—again!

Divide and replant your irises and give many away to friends.

Continue to dead-head annuals.

Begin to make cages for protecting precious plants from deer, rabbits, and the like. You never can be too early or have too many.

Check your evergreens for armyworms.

Keep the birdbath full of water.

Repair fences.

Continue the attack on Japanese beetles.

Remember to cultivate the perennial border.

If you have a woodlot or some woods, start cutting now for next winter's use.

Take some pictures of the garden in bloom to look at with wonder when the snow is flying.

Collect seeds from the rock garden.

NOTES

A garden that one makes oneself becomes associated with one's personal history and that of one's friends, interwoven with one's tastes, preferences and character, and constitutes a sort of unwritten but withal manifest, autobiography. Show me your garden, provided it be your own, and I will tell you what you are like. It is in middle life that the finishing touches should be put to it; and then, after that, it should remain more or less in the same condition, like oneself, growing more deep of shade, and more protected from the winds....

ALFRED AUSTIN

My father still goes out every spring and he's now eighty and plants an apple tree. Next year he plans on starting oaks...now that's really faith!

ANONYMOUS

Fall creeps in on little cat feet: Gradually the nights are cooler, stars brighter; leaves have lost the green of youth, becoming tired as the days roll by; crickets chirp continually now, never stopping their chorus until the frosts of October; autumn chores begin.

NATURALIZING NARCISSUS AND DAFFODILS

Back in the spring we talked about naturalizing bulbs, and now is the time to act. Plant the bulbs as soon as you receive them—never let them lie about in paper bags and be forgotten; before you know it, they will sprout and all will be lost.

Go outside and scatter the bulbs at random, planting them where they fall in order to achieve a completely natural look. In ground that has never been planted before, dig a hole that is three times the diameter of the bulb (a two-inch bulb goes into a six-inch hole). Special bulb planters in both trowel and shovel form are available should your plantings be a major effort.

THE SILVER-LACE VINE

If you have a wall, fence, or trellis that begs to be covered with a fast growth of leaves and flowers, the silver-lace vine *(Polygonum aubertii)* is the perfect answer. The small flowers that cover twining stems with great abundance become a white haze from a distance, completely hiding the leaves from view. Also called the "China fleece vine," the plants are billed as one of the fastest growing vines in existence, reaching fifteen to twenty feet in length (or height) in the first season, and it's a true claim.

BEAUTIFUL COSMOS

For cut flowers of unsurpassed beauty coupled with a clean, brisk charm, choose the annual cosmos *(Cosmos bipinnatus)*. Especially attractive in both bowl and border are the "Sensation" variety, the pink and the white. If plants are grown in a reasonably good soil and given a few doses of plant food over the summer, you will get flowers up to five inches across on plants that could top six feet in height. If able, start seeds indoors for earlier bloom, and always remove dead flowers before seeds are set. The colored petals are really modified leaves; the true flowers are the small parts of the yellow centers. The drawing shows the white form.

The vines are harmless to foundations, walls, and brick mortar—unlike ivies and the like—because they cling by twining about and not by utilizing suckers. They like a warm and sunny spot—this is not a candidate for the shade. The vine in the drawing grows on a bamboo arbor.

Make sure you buy container-grown plants for faster growth; bare-root vines will take a few weeks to settle in before they snap out of their self-imposed lethargy. Give them a reasonably good soil for a start, since once this vine is established, you will never get it out of that spot again.

THE SECOND FRENCH CALENDAR

After the French Revolution, the first French Republic decided to remake the calendar and solve the problems of twelve months that had uneven numbers of days and, at the same time, sweep away all vestiges of the previous ruling ethic. With typical French verve, they did away entirely with weeks, dividing the months into three decades, every tenth day *(décadi)* being a day of rest. There were twelve months of thirty days each, with five remaining days called "feast days" and named for Virtue, Genius, Labor, Reason, and Reward. In leap years, the last day of the year was the extra day and called Revolution Day.

The English, with their typical reserve, thought the whole thing was silly beyond belief and gave the French months snide names of their own. Names and dates are listed below with English equivalents in parentheses.

1. *Vendémiaire*	Vintage month	(Wheezy)	9/22–10/22
2. *Brumaire*	Fog	(Sneezy)	10/23–11/20
3. *Frimaire*	Sleet	(Freezy)	11/21–12/20
4. *Nivôse*	Snow	(Slippy)	12/21– 1/19
5. *Pluviôse*	Rain	(Drippy)	1/20– 2/18
6. *Ventôse*	Wind	(Nippy)	2/19– 3/20
7. *Germinal*	Seed	(Showery)	3/21– 4/19
8. *Floréal*	Blossom	(Flowery)	4/20– 5/19
9. *Prairial*	Pasture	(Bowery)	5/20– 6/18
10. *Messidor*	Harvest	(Wheaty)	6/19– 7/18
11. *Thermidor*	Heat	(Heaty)	7/19– 8/17
12. *Fructidor*	Fruit	(Sweety)	8/18– 9/16

The system lasted from 1793 to 1805.

THE TRUMPET VINE

Here's another blooming vine to cover an unsightly wall, twine along a fence, climb a trellis or even an ugly utility pole. It's called the "trumpet vine" *(Bignonia capreolata)* but is often listed under the incorrect name *Campsis*. It's hardy to zone 5, although basically known as a more southern plant. Temporary fastening will be needed for the first year until the vine gets itself established: Use patented vine anchors or twist ties.

Plants prefer full sun and should be planted in good, rich soil so they get off to a healthy start. Once settled in, vines quickly send out leaders; if it goes too far for you, clip them off.

Flowers are trumpet-shaped and glow in red and orange.

THE FASTEST VINE

The silver-lace vine is the answer to an impatient gardener's prayer. One summer of growth will yield fifteen to twenty feet of twining stems. The flowers have a delicate and lacy quality but the vine itself is very strong and will quickly cover a multitude of sins.

In addition to the common variety, there is one other cultivar available, *B. capreolata* **'Crimson Trumpet'**, with more flowers and a brighter color.

The other trumpet vines often found listed with the previous types are: *Campsis radicans,* the yellow trumpet vine; and *C.* × *Tagliabuana* **'Mme. Galen'**, with very large trumpet-shaped flowers of apricot-orange.

Plant these vines close enough to an area of relaxed seating so you can watch the hummingbirds.

HOGWEED IS COMING, HOGWEED IS COMING!

From out of the steppes of central Asia — naturally from the Russians — comes the latest scourge to hit the plant world: the Kung-fu of the flower kingdom, the stationary kudzu, the giant hogweed!

Known as *Heracleum Mantegazzianum,* this statuesque member of the lowly parsley family has had a home in my garden for a number of years, grown with seed obtained from England. In our backyard it's never topped twelve feet in height—but a botanist up in Vancouver, B.C., reports his plant next to the front door topped twenty feet in its first year of growth.

Short or tall, this imposing plant has been grown for decoration in England for years, but unfortunately escaped from cultivation, invading Battersea Park and other sites around London. Now it's doing the same in the States — but note: The first infestation was reported in western New York where it probably spread from Highland Park in Rochester, having been grown there as an ornamental since 1917.

Well, what's the problem? The stems of this beauty are hollow and roughly one inch thick. Each stem section can be up to two feet in length, in short a perfect peashooter. In addition, the sap contains a chemical, psoralen, which — when exposed to sunlight — produces a painful irritation known as phytophotodermatitis, a blistering affair. If a victim isn't careful, the blisters may become infected; and following the blisters, disfiguring brown marks appear on the skin that may last for months.

Since the plant is a biennial, it will only grow leaves the first year, flower the second, then die. I've always kept it under control by cutting off the flower head before the seeds form, keeping only a few for the next year in the garden.

Because the sap is activated by sunlight, it is advised that you cut it down on a cloudy day or at night.

It makes a wonderful addition to a dried winter bouquet and does look well in the wilder part of the garden. Just warn the kids.

THE OBEDIENT PLANT

One of the garden flowers that refuses to give up the ghost as autumn rolls around is the obedient plant *(Physostegia virginiana).* The flowers will not begin to bloom until well into September and have a tenacious knack of surviving frost. Flower spikes will grow

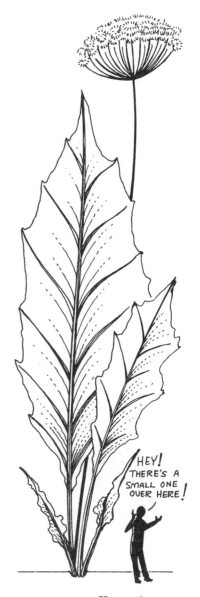

HEY! THERE'S A SMALL ONE OVER HERE!

Hogweed

THE TRUMPET VINE
   A hummingbird swoops down on a blossom in the drawing at left.

Obedient plant

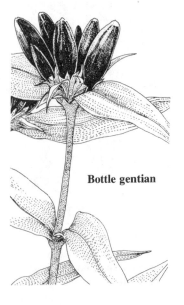

Bottle gentian

up to three feet tall in good garden soil and get their name from each blossom's movement on the stem: Push them about and they will remain in the last position until you give them another tap with a finger.

Physostegia has to be watched in the garden as it can easily spread by creeping roots, but it is excellent for that certain damp location where many other plants refuse to succeed.

The white form of *Physostegia,* **'Alba'**, is not quite as weedy and is considered more demure than the rose-magenta of the typical flower. It's not as tough and needs better drainage. A variegated form is sometimes offered by out-of-the-way nurseries.

Propagation of all is by division or seed.

THE BOTTLE GENTIAN

One of the most interesting flowers of the autumn season is the closed, blind, or bottle gentian *(Gentiana andrewsii),* which blooms in September and October, usually in slightly acid, somewhat moist soil, and in a spot that offers partial shade. There are always plants that refuse to follow the rules and you might find a clump of these beauties in the midst of a sunny field, partially protected by tall grasses.

The deep and intense blue of this gentian is reason enough to grow it—a colony of them is a thrill to the eye. But the fact that an unopened flower is pollinated by bees makes them a fitting subject of a lesson in natural history. Since I could never equal the prose of Neltje Blanchan in the 1904 edition of *Nature's Garden,* I quote the following description:

> **How can a bumblebee enter this inhospitable-looking flower? If he did but know it, it keeps closed for his special benefit, having no fringes or hairs to entangle the feet of crawling pilferers, and no better way of protecting its nectar from rain and marauding butterflies that are not adapted to its needs. But he is a powerful fellow. Watch him alight on a cluster of blossoms, select the younger, nectar-bearing ones, that are distinctly marked white against a light-blue background at the mouth of the [blossom] for his special guidance. Old flowers from which the nectar has been removed turn deep reddish-purple, and the white pathfinders become indistinct. With some difficulty, it is true, the bumblebee thrusts his tongue through the valve of the chosen flower where the five lobes overlap one another; then he pushes with all his might until his head having passed the entrance most of his body follows, leaving only his hind legs and the tip of his abdomen sticking out as he makes the circuit. He has much sense as well as muscle, and does not risk imprisonment in what must prove a tomb by a total and unnecessary disappearance within the bottle. Presently he backs out, brushes the pollen from his head...into his [pollen] baskets, and is off to fertilize an older flower with the few grains of dust that must remain on his velvety head.**

Every once in a while, the spirit of Nature indulges in a bit of carelessness and a white-flowered form of the bottle gentian is produced.

BRINGING IN THE FIG

This wonderful tree with its legendary fruit has been in cultivation for centuries. Properly ripened figs are not only sweet and delicious but nutritious as well. From zone 7 on up, the common fig *(Ficus carica)* can stay outside. During the dormant period, it can even withstand temperatures of 10°F.; but when sprouting, anything freezing or below can severely damage new growth. Fruit develops on the branch tips of one- and two-year-old wood. In warmer climates where there is plenty of time for development, they will mature in one step. If, because of tolerated cold, dormancy sets in, the crop will develop the next season.

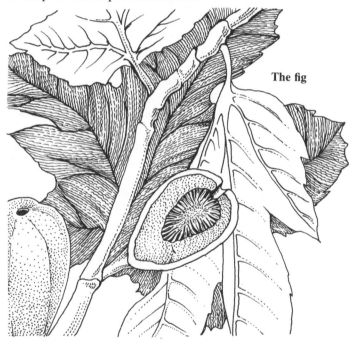

The fig

Figs are unusual in that the flowers are never seen; they are on the inside of the fruit, and in many varieties a tiny wasp climbs in at the base of the fig to pollinate the flower.

Figs make great pot plants in nine- to twelve-inch pots, using a soil mix of one-third good potting soil, one-third peat, and one-third sharp sand. Be sure to provide adequate water, and fertilize with a liquid plant food every three weeks during active growth. Repot in the fall with new soil, or at least topdress the existing soil.

After your potted fig has enjoyed a season in the sun, allow it to be exposed to a few frosts to start dormancy, then put it in a cool basement till spring, or bring into 65°F. and start growth again.

The hardiest variety and the one best suited for indoor growth is the "Brown Turkey" cultivar.

PARSLEY

Parsley *(Petroselinum crispum)* is a time-honored herb that every restaurant deems important to drop atop each sliced or whole potato. But it's much better chopped or shredded in salads, especially when you gather sprigs in the dead of winter from your sunny windowsill, or added to otherwise bland cottage cheese.

The plants are biennial and difficult to germinate. Soak seeds in water for twenty-four hours before planting since they are notoriously slow to germinate, often taking six weeks. Running on the assumption that you or a friend grew some in your vegetable gardens, dig up roots in the fall and bring indoors to that sunny kitchen window.

BRINGING IN THE PLANTS

Always be careful when you bring plants in from the outside after their summer vacation in the open air. Pests abound and it's unfair to infect other houseplants when it can easily be avoided. Don't bring pots directly into general contact; keep them isolated for about two weeks so you can spot insects or diseases before they start to run rampant.

Special honors go to the spider mite for damage above and beyond the call. Mites are extremely tiny but can be seen by a normal pair of eyes as small specks marching up and down *the undersurface* of a leaf. Once they become established, the female lays about a hundred eggs during a two-week cycle, and each of these will hatch and produce another hundred, and on and on and on....

The first signs of damage are small, dried-out areas that appear on the top of the leaf. Soon the entire leaf browns and dies, but not before the undersurface is covered by tiny, crisscrossed webs. These webs make control difficult as they protect both eggs and mites from being dislodged by a strong flow of water, the cure usually cited.

Mites like it warm and dry, so cool and damp surroundings will slow them down. Daily mistings help, too. But the only tried and safe method that I've found is soap and water, with weekly applications. Once is not enough as you're bound to miss either a few mites or a few eggs.

The first step is to isolate the infected plant. Before soaping, cover the soil with a layer of aluminum foil to keep dirt from falling out; a little soap won't hurt the plant. If too large for the kitchen sink, move to the bathtub. Now, lather up and completely cover the leaves and stems with soapsuds. If leaves are tender, carefully massage with your fingertips; if leaves are tougher, then a small brush won't hurt. After the suds have sat on the leaves for about five minutes, rinse everything off. Repeat the process in ten days to two weeks.

As I am writing this book, a new product has appeared on the market: a ready-to-use insecticidal soap that is *not* washed off the leaves. Unfortunately, it's too early for product reports yet.

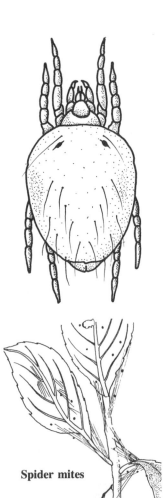

Spider mites

THE LIGULARIAS

This morning the ground in the garden has the consistency and look of an overabundant chocolate *mousse,* and one conjures up visions of sinking into a sea of mordant peat or at best a flooded swamp. Even so the autumn garden is alive with color and now at the end of September we've yet to have a killing frost to 'do it in.'

One of the prize flowers of the early fall is the ligularia, a member of the daisy family that originally hailed from China and if offered just a modicum of winter protection will do quite well in zone 5.

Ligularia

This handsome plant prefers ample moisture and a reasonably fertile soil. They are easily divided in early spring but show the effects of droughty conditions if deprived of water during active growth.

Ligularias will produce a very large clump of vegetation and send up erect spikes of orange-yellow flowers — quite like huge daisies—beginning to bloom in early fall and persisting until they perish under a major frost. Pictured is *Ligularia dentata* **'Desdemona'**.

In addition to spectacular flowers, they offer leaves that are a treat in themselves. Purple in early spring they only begin turning green as they open. In a well-established plant, some leaves can attain a width of twelve inches so allow plenty of garden room for expansion.

Three species are usually offered for sale in the United States: *Ligularia dentata* **'Desdemona'** is the species described and in addition to the features cited, the flowers possess a fresh and distinctive fragrance. *L. stenocephala* **'The Rocket'** has a coarser leaf edge and grows to six feet in a good year. *L. Hodgsonii* blooms earlier in the year and only reaches a height of two to three feet.

SURPRISES IN THE MAIL

Every fall, a gardener friend of mine sets aside the workaday world and goes on a gardener's vacation, aiming his sights on the mountains of Colorado, New Mexico, and finally on Washington, collecting plants from other gardeners on his way or seeds from plants in the wild. At the end of two weeks, my friend has dozens of plants for his garden and the donors have struck up acquaintances for their own future treks across America and Canada.

The nice thing about gardeners in general, and my friend in particular, is the aforementioned generosity, and this past year was no exception. Waiting for me at the post office last Monday morning was a small — but heavy — package, festooned with stamps and bearing a return address from an obscure mining town in Colorado, close to Our Gal Sunday's.

I hurried home, hating to wait for the ceremony of tearing the masking tape and pulling the package apart, then carefully unwrapping each crumpled piece of foil that surrounded a tiny but fresh-as-a-daisy plant donated by a gardener of many years' standing.

By joining any number of specialty societies in North America (and England and Europe), a whole world of gardeners is opened to your experience — and I state again: They are the most generous people in the world.

Join one today and share in the experience!

HINTS FOR SEPTEMBER

Start to bring your houseplants indoors again. Watch for pests.

Ready all bird feeders for the coming winter.

Continue to cultivate the border and weed with a vengeance.

Keep plastic sheets, screens, large pots, cloches, etc., ready for the first frosts.

Always put a piece of screening over the hole in a pot to prevent the earthworm and other visitors from coming in with your houseplants.

Keep on watering, especially if the season is dry. All plants need water to enter winter dormancy in good health.

Cut flowers to dry for winter bouquets.

Spend a sunny afternoon washing pots.

If you are extending the garden, dig and turn over the soil now so the winter continues to break down the earth.

Get ready to chase the deer and rabbits.

Clean all your tools for storage.

Rake leaves for compost — never burn them!

Plant mums for fall bloom.

Notes

Walked for half an hour in the garden. A fine rain was falling, and the landscape was that of autumn. The sky was hung with various shades of gray, and mists hovered about the distant mountains—a melancholy nature. The leaves were falling on all sides like the last illusions of youth under the tears of irremediable grief. A brood of chattering birds were chasing each other through the shrubberies, and playing games among the branches, like a knot of hiding schoolboys. Every landscape is, as it were, a state of the soul, and whoever penetrates into both is astonished to find how much likeness there is in each detail.

HENRI FREDERIC AMIEL
(Translated by Mrs. Humphry Ward)

It's now the middle of October, the leaves have been driven from the trees, and snow flurries are predicted for tomorrow. Nights are cold, and the ice is on the birdbath water every morning until melted by the midmorning sun; the geese have long flown and the gleaners* have continued their flights to the South as they follow and gather leftovers from the fall harvests; so how does the garden grow?

Surprisingly, there are a number of flowers: The American sunflower *(Helianthus giganteus)* is still a mass of yellow blooms on its nine-foot stalks, bright against the cloudy sky and at close quarters exuding a wonderful odor of chocolate; the New England asters *(Aster novae-angliae)* dot the perennial border with shades of blue and deep purple; and though I confess to moving the geraniums inside every night, they are outside again every reasonably warm morning to brighten their corner.

Farther along the border, blue ladybells *(Adenophora Farreri)* are now producing their third crop of flowers atop two-foot stems (except those that my dear friends the deer have chosen to nibble off) and the dwarf goldenrod *(Solidago spathulata* var. *nana)* dot the ground with tiny yellow stars.

Up in the rock garden, the cinquefoil *(Potentilla parvifolia* **'Gold Drop')** sports ten to fifteen new flowers every day, and a few of the dwarf sedums *(Sedum* cultivars) still bear tiny bunches of rosy-red blossoms.

Next to the waving plumes of the zebra grass *(Miscanthus sinensis* **'Zebrinus')**, the blazing-star *(Liatris scariosa)* is covered

THE TOAD LILY

From Japan comes another strange and valued garden dweller, the toad lily *(Tricyrtis hirta)*. Pointed leaves on arching stems are attractive in the garden from spring to fall, but the unusual happens in October when mauve and purple flowers bloom within the leaf axils and stem tops, each with a split pistil that closely resembles the texture of chenille. Plants like a semishady spot with moist soil, and it's a good idea to use a mulch north of zone 5. Propagation is by division or seeds.

*A local name for the slate-colored junco *(Junco hyemalis).*

117

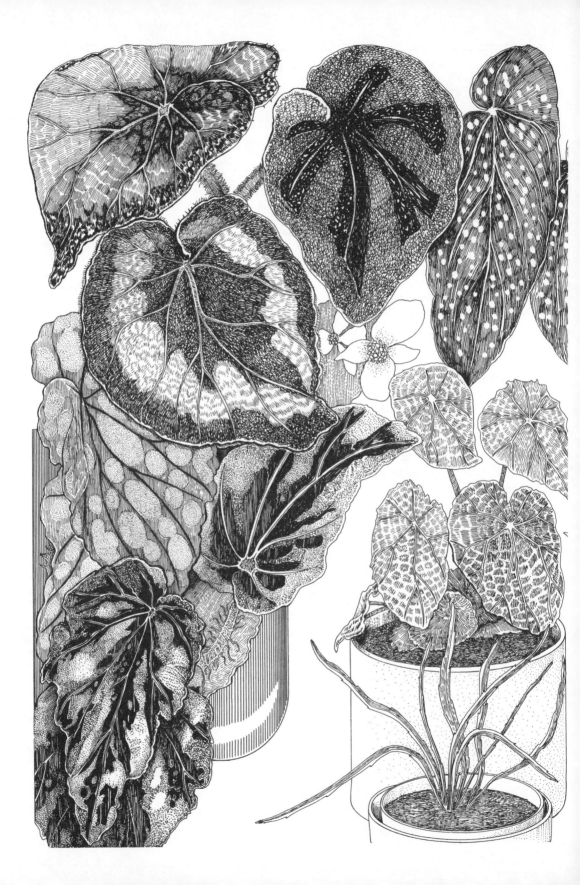

with its white and fluffy disklike flowers. It's an odd flower since the blooming begins at the top and proceeds down the stem as opposed to most other plants, and an excellent choice for bouquets since by clipping off the old flowers the spike looks almost new every time. Obviously the garden is far from over....

THE BEGONIA TRIBE

The drawing on the preceding pages shows just some of the variety to be expected when exploring the begonia tribe. There are many variations in cultural requirements, too; but on the average, plants prefer temperatures between 58°F. and 72°F., a higher humidity level (between 40 percent and 60 percent) than is usually found in the average home, bright light all year long (with the general exception of hot sun at midday in July and August), and a good potting mix that is coarse in texture, light in weight, and porous to allow for good drainage yet able to hold enough moisture to keep roots moist. There are so many different mixes that the best plan is to follow the advice — always freely given — of your place of supply.

FLORAL HELPS AND HINTS

A friend stopped by the other day with a book entitled *A Pictorial Scrapbook* (sold for 12¢ back in 1898), beautifully bound and full of clippings that her uncle had gathered from the *Ladies' Home Journal* from 1896 to 1900. Each clipping was carefully cut and pasted to the page, and all concerned "Floral Helps and Hints" penned by Eben E. Rexford.

I began to read and found myself impressed with the knowledge gathered by Mr. Rexford and the forthright way he answered questions from his magazine audience. But another quality was found in these pasted tracts: a marvelous independence and desire to experiment; the professional was consulted only when the amateur failed, and not before!

The following letter, entitled *Worms in Begonias,* along with Rexford's answer, was written in 1897:

> ...I used lime-water for months. The plants were not benefited by it, and the worms were not injured by it, Then I tried thrusting parlor matches into the soil. I used the matches unsparingly, often twelve to twenty in a pot. When the phosphorus was washed off more matches were used, and all water than ran through the saucers was poured back upon the soil. In my desire to destroy the worms I lost sight of possible destruction of the plants, so I proceeded quite recklessly with my experiment. In a short time the worms were washed up by applications of water, and they were no longer wriggling, squirming, defiant things, but dead as the proverbial door nail. Now every begonia is looking its best. In fact, my plants have never looked as healthy as the present. I shall pin my faith to matches henceforth when I start out to fight worms. I have been told by persons who have used matches that they were ineffective. I now believe that not enough of

A BEVY OF BEGONIAS

The begonias in the drawing are clockwise from top left *Begonia* 'Queen Mother', *Begonia* 'Iron Cross', *B. maculata, B. diadema, B. polygonoides, B. partita, B. bogneri, Begonia* 'Venetian Red', *Begonia "ex-Kew species,"* and *Begonia* 'Queen of Hanover'.

them were used. I went in for heroic treatment, and the results were entirely satisfactory to me and to my plants.

Mr. Rexford's reply: "Begonias drop their leaves from several causes, prominent among which is poor drainage. Always see that there is ample opportunity for surplus water to run off at the bottom of the pots. Too much water about the roots—stagnant water—soon results in disease, and one of the first symptoms of defective root action is the dropping of leaves."

In this case I assume that Mr. Rexford was so awe-struck by the letter, he was unable to comment on the worms and immediately changed the subject.

BRING IN THE FUCHSIA

One of the outstanding plants for summer's hanging baskets is the fuchsia, with its number of species and cultivars, and it's a shame to toss out the plants at season's end. Instead, winter the plants in your basement as close to the magic 40°F. temperature as you can. Water them once a month, just enough to keep the old wood from drying out and the soil becoming rock-hard. In February, when days are noticeably longer, bring the plants up to a sunny window, wait for the first green buds to emerge, and then prune back the branches to at least half their length. Fuchsias only bloom on new growth, so this is necessary to produce flowers. Repot the plant in new soil (one-half potting soil, one-quarter composted manure, and one-quarter sharp sand) and a pot one size larger than present. Fuchsias need additional help with food once blooming starts in earnest, so use a liquid plant food every three weeks during the summer and never let plants completely dry out.

A fuchsia bloom

GARDEN SEDUMS

Along the roadsides and on steep banks and hills, the goldenrod is now in full bloom; and farther north than I, it's already on the wane. Its sweep of yellow dominates the view unless shared with the purple of the wild asters.

In many area gardens, however, it's a different story as the dozen or so varieties of *Sedum* are now in full flower. Sedums are members of the same family as the common jade plant of indoor-garden lore and have been cultivated in gardens for centuries. The name (from the Latin *sedo,* to calm or allay) dates back to the Roman era when the smaller members of the clan were grown on house roofs because folks believed that these plants would keep lightning away.

The leaves are fleshy and able to withstand long periods of drought. Indeed they demand well-drained soil, and although tolerant of poor fertility, the richer the soil, the better they will grow.

Flower heads start to form in the middle of summer and remain one of the best parts of the plants, glowing with greenish-white patterns until most begin their long period of bloom in early fall.

They are perfectly hardy in zone 4, will even grow well in pots, and make admirable cut flowers, most beautiful when left to themselves in a vase.

The shorter types like *Sedum Kamtschaticum* and *S. ternatum* are fine additions to the rock garden, while the larger types are best in the perennial border. *S. maximum* **'Atropurpureum'** and *S. Telephium* **'Autumn Joy'** are especially pretty, with creamy-rose flowers in the first, and a deep rust-color in the second.

Sedums propagate with ease by division and are not prone to any major diseases or insect pests.

FLOWERING KALE

If you've never seen or grown a pot or plant of ornamental kale *(Brassica oleracea* var. *acephala),* what a treat's in store! Not really a flower at all, the rippled and colorful "blossom" is really a type of cabbage with leaves for the rosette unlike the more typical tightly packed vegetable head.

They're now pop plants with florists in many northern urban areas, where potted singles sell for $15 and up, depending on the size—and a well-grown plant can be two feet tall and two feet wide, or even more.

You can have your own by starting at the season's beginning with seeds, planted in a good soil, transplanted to the outdoors for the summer with plenty of water and full sun, then potted up in early fall. Use a heavy soil mix as these plants are so heavy they can easily topple out.

Leaf colors are the best when temperatures hover around 40°F.

Cut stems with heads can be put into water. Remove the lower leaves as they fade and cut off the bottom stem as the top continues to expand and lengthen.

Flowering kale

Four hybrids are now available: the new frizzy red or frizzy white, with curled and tightly laced leaf edges that resemble crocheting; and the more traditional red on green or white on green.

While many sources claim they are good to eat, the leaves are tougher than the plain green types and flavor is not too good. Remember to check your plants with care before bringing them indoors, just in case a wandering cabbage caterpillar has taken up residence in your floral decorations.

"In this box you have every thing you need to grow, harvest, and thoroughly enjoy mushrooms. With Farm-in-a-Box you just add water, follow the easy instructions, and in 3 to 4 weeks, you'll harvest your first crop of plump, delicious mushrooms—ready to serve raw or in your favorite recipe," so says the brochure that comes with this fascinating new introduction to growing gourmet food in the home!

And it works. Everything you need is really in one box. The only requirements are a temperature range between 55° and 75°F., no danger from freezing, adequate protection from drafts, and dry surroundings.

You can actually watch the mushrooms grow, and if properly handled, a typical farm will produce mushrooms for two to three months.

We tried it at our house and the raves were unanimous.

STEAL A MARCH ON SPRING

In a wonderful newspaper from Wolcott, Indiana, I found the following information on tomatoes that I pass along for those vegetable growers among us.

Before the first killing frost nips them, pick those tomatoes that are nearing maturity and clean and wash them. Then wrap each in a piece of newspaper or waxed paper, but do not seal the ends. Place them on a tray and put all in a cool, unlighted area where the temperature does not fall below 55°F. Check the tomatoes every few days to determine those ready for use and discard any damaged or decaying fruit.

Green tomatoes may also be stored by selecting green fruit and washing with a weak solution of disinfectant, such as household bleach. Prepare the disinfectant by adding one teaspoon of bleach to a quart of water. Dry thoroughly, wrap in newspapers, and store in a cool area.

If all else fails (and you have the room to spare), pull the vines up whole and hang them in cool surroundings. The fruit will slowly ripen over a long period of time.

Another plant that responds to this hanging approach is the garden geranium. If you can't winter over plants in a cool, sunny window, simply pull the entire plant out of the ground, shake off the loose soil, and hang the plant upside down in a cool, dry attic, garage, or basement. Replant outdoors in early spring when frosts are past.

Since many good things come in threes, the final plant to respond to this treatment is the garden four-o-clock, or miracle of Peru. This charming plant, usually sold as an annual, is in reality a perennial. If the plants are dug up in the fall, you'll find a large tuber instead of many loose roots. Rub off the excess dirt, let the tubers dry in a warm place for a few days, then store them along with the geraniums and tomatoes for next year. Your plants will grow twice as large as the neighbors' and bloom weeks earlier.

A FAVORITE HOUSEPLANT

Recently a friend asked about the care and nurture of a fairly popular houseplant known as the false aralia, threadleaf, or, by those in the know; Dizzy. The Latin name is *Dizygotheca elegantissima,* giving rise to the nickname and also underlining the point that this is a beautiful and elegant plant.

Originally discovered in the New Hebrides Islands about 1870, this shrub will eventually grow into a small tree of some twenty-five feet in height, but usually not in the average home.

Confusion began some years ago over the various stages of life in Dizzy. When young and in the shrub form, leaves are compound on long, dark-green-and-white mottled stems, the seven to ten arching leaflets toothed and graceful. At maturity, the leaf character changes: Leaflets become lance-shaped, generally broader, and the tooth turns to lobe. For a while scientists were concerned over the true identity of the plant; but with diligent observations, they sorted it out.

Winter temperatures should be between 55° and 60°F. The foliage needs moist air in order to retain its beauty and color—dry air will quickly shrivel and brown the leaf edges. Mist the leaves on a regular basis and keep the plant from the hot, direct rays of the summer sun.

Water normally in summer, providing a good houseplant fertilizer on a monthly basis. Cut back on water in the winter as the plants need a rest.

The worst pest is the spider mite (see p. 112).

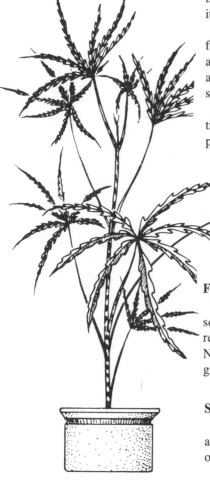

Dizygotheca elegantissima

FRESH DANDELIONS FOR WINTER

Before the ground freezes up, go out into the yard and dig up some dandelion roots. Plant them in a heavy cardboard box, using regular garden dirt, and leave the box outdoors until it's frozen. Now bring indoors to a warm spot and the dandelions will begin to grow with succulent and great-tasting leaves.

SALT HAY AND PINE NEEDLES

Two of the finest mulches for winterizing the garden are salt hay and pine needles. Generally, if you have one, you won't have the other—and vice versa.

Salt hay is hay that's been grown and cut in salt marshes. It's extremely valuable for mulching because the stems are likely to remain firm, not likely to mat and freeze together; it's usually weed-free; and it can be used year after year. Fresh hay is never quite as good.

Pine needles are superb as mulch: They allow water to leak through, provide good air circulation, and are extremely durable. If you've ever walked in a pinewoods in July and felt the earth beneath the layer of fallen needles, you will know about the fine insulation they provide.

Other mulches usually available at nurseries and garden centers are buckwheat hulls, peanut shells in the South, peat moss, sawdust, and wood chips.

Eschew Styrofoam packing pellets and black plastics and polyethylene: They do not belong in a garden dedicated to life.

There is virtue in the open, there is
healing out of doors;
The great Physician makes his rounds
along the forest floors.
Have little care that life is brief,
And less that art is long.
Success is in the silences
Though fame is in the song.
BLISS CARMEN

Cyclamen

HINTS FOR OCTOBER

Unless you are very lucky, the frost will soon be here (if it hasn't arrived already) so be on the alert to cover precious plants.

Bring some mums indoors for brightening up the rooms.

Watch for moles and their tunnels.

Bring in gladiolus and dahlias for winter storage.

Bring in those garden ornaments that might be shattered by frost and freezing.

Get pine needles and salt hay ready for winter mulching.

Label any plants that you have forgotten or you will truly forget by next year.

Continue to weed.

Don't forget to shut off the outdoor water before pipes break.

Check and rewind the hose for next year.

Tie up or trim the climbing roses on the arbor.

Last call to plant bulbs for next spring's bloom.

Watch indoor plants for whitefly, red spider, and mealybugs.

Continue to weed.

Take a walk through the garden and make the beginnings of a plan for next year.

Notes

The leaves are gone from the trees . . . the wild geese
have flown . . . Thanksgiving is not far off . . .

I've never sailed the Amazon,
  I've never reached Brazil;
But the *Don* and *Magdalena*,
  They can go there when they will!
Yes, weekly from Southampton,
Great steamers, white and gold,
Go rolling down to Rio
(Roll down—roll down to Rio!).
And I'd like to roll to Rio
Someday before I'm old!
   RUDYARD KIPLING

From the gardener's point of view, November can be the worst
month to be faced: Nature is winding things down, the air is cold,
skies are gray, but usually the final mark of punctuation to the year
has yet to arrive—the snow; snow that covers all in the garden and
marks a mind-set for the end of a year's activity. There is little to do
outside except to wait for longer days in the new year and the joys of
the coming holidays.

WOOD ASH FOR THE GARDEN

Since many gardeners now heat most or some of their homes
with wood, the question arises: Are the ashes safe for the garden?

Wood ashes are alkaline and raise the pH of the soil in the same
way that ground limestone will. According to the variety, ashes also contain minerals: 6 percent potash, about 18 percent calcium,
2 percent phosphoric acid, plus small amounts of sulfur and mag-
nesium.

One cord of seasoned wood yields about twenty pounds of ash,
just enough to cover 1,000 square feet of garden if the soil is too
acid.

PEARLY EVERLASTING

If you had been fortunate enough to plant a clump of this
attractive wildflower last summer, it would now be evident as a
white bouquet shining in the midst of your garden, unharmed by
rains or frost, and waiting for the coming mantle of snow. For the
petals of everlastings have the ability to dry like tough paper and
remain forever pure and durable.

THE BEAUTIFUL OXALIS

Members of the *Oxalis* genus
make wonderful houseplants.
Their fresh green three-lobed
leaves strike a cheerful note on
any sunny windowsill. They are
not particular as to soil mixes—
any well-drained medium will
work. All like good light, and
many species are excellent in
hanging baskets. The flowers
are large and colorful, open
only in the sunlight and close up
for the night. All species with
thickened rootstocks go into a
dormant period after bloom.
The plant at left, *Oxalis Bowiei*,
produces leaves some four
inches wide with rosy-red flowers in late summer and fall.

There are two schools of thought on this everlasting quality: Neltje Blanchan (in his famous turn-of-the-century book) said: "An imaginary blossom that never fades has been the dream of poets from Milton's day; but seeing one, who loves it? Our [flower] has the aspect of an artificial [bloom] — stiff, dry, soulless, quite in keeping with the decorations on the average farmhouse mantel-piece—a wreath about flowers made from the lifeless hair of some dear departed."

James Edward Smith in his book of English botany said: "This flower, from its purity and durability, is an elegant emblem of immortality and is a common favorite in cottage gardens. . . where it is most beautiful."

So, as with most things of this world, there are two schools of thought.

I still like the flower, not only in the garden but in those dried arrangements for the winter table. The petals are really modified leaves; the true flowers are the tiny yellow or brown florets in the center of each bloom. The stems are covered with a cottony substance meant to keep wandering ants from stealing the nectar kept only for small bees and flies.

The wild type is called *Anaphalis margaritacea.* A more genteel type from the Himalyas is shorter in stature and called *A. triplinervis.* Clumps are easily divided and moved, but it's best to do it in the early spring. The attractive gray-green leaf color of both species looks well in the summer garden, long before the blossoms appear.

Flower heads were once used as the ingredients of expectorants in treating colds, but this seems to have been out of favor for centuries.

Pearly everlasting

Although the stems of the Stapeliads—and stems they are, for the leaves are tiny or minuscule — have never been the hit of the houseplant world, the flowers are. Bizarre, unique, and indelicate, they always elicit response when displayed at flower shows, generating choruses of Ohhs and ahhhs when plants accompany me on lectures.

"I'd call it a crochet flower," said one lady. "They don't look real —a creation of hook and needle, I'd say."

"A strange hook and needle," said her husband.

"But worth having in the collection," added another lady. "Could I have a cutting?"

Everyone wants a cutting. Then when all the guests have been provided with a bit of stem, they ask about the odor associated with the plant's common name of carrion flower. It isn't bad, I explain, only getting very strong when you have a multitude of flowers in a closed room or you push a nose too close to the blooms.

The odor is necessary since these plants mostly grow in the desert and dry areas of South Africa where bees are definitely in the minority, so everything is set up to attract a fly. This fly spots a typical flower from the air and, like the bee, is attracted first by the colors of the petals and then by the odor produced by the small glands responsible for the flower's nectar. Unlike the gaudy and flagrant colors of most flowers, stapelias tend to ochre, mauve, and purple tones, often with a dash of yellow—colors made for a fly.

Seed

Rudimentary leaf

Offset

Roots

Stapeliads

These plants are all succulents, so the primary rule of care is: Provide adequate drainage. I use a soil mix of one-third sharp sand, one-third standard potting soil, and one-third well-rotted manure, with a liberal sprinkling of small charcoal chips and gravel.

While most will endure a temperature of 40°F., they do not like such a chilly atmostphere. If allowed to sit in wet soil when the temperature falls that low, they will usually begin to rot. I withhold water from November to March, moving the plants up to my study where the temperature fluctuates between 50° and 70°F., depending on the outside winds and the use of the room.

The only serious pest is the mealybug. To eliminate this beast, use swabs with alcohol touched directly to the insect's body. For severe infestations, sterilize the soil and wash stems and roots in denatured alcohol for a few minutes, then rinse in warm water before replanting.

Bamboos conjure up visions of steamy jungles, orange orangu-tans, exotic fruits, and very comfortable temperatures. Yet today is bleak—gray sky, about 20°F.—and, believe it or not, branches of bamboo are peeking up with gracefully sculptured leaves through the foot of snow outside our door.

A number of bamboos are able to exist in very cold climates as they originally hail from the northern mountains of Japan and the peaks of central China. *Arundinaria murielae*—first collected in China by Ernest Wilson—is hardy down to −20°F. and will live in areas colder than that if given a mulch of straw or a season-long blanket of snow. *Sasa nitida,* also from China is hardy to zone 6.

The pygmy bamboo *(A. pygmaea)* is the smallest of all the bamboos and in addition to making an excellent ground cover with its eight- to ten-inch height — easily cut by a lawn mower if it spreads too far for comfort—makes a desirable houseplant. There is a variegated cultivar *(A. pygmaea variegata)* that is even more attractive both indoors and out.

Bamboos grown indoors have only one fault: They drop leaves in the fall. They quickly recover, however, as days get longer and temperatures warm up. They all grow easily from seed, and if you get involved in specialization and collecting, a large number of species are at your beck and call.

A MAP OF THE GARDEN

When winter snows cover the ground, there is no better time to take up pencil or pen and proceed with a map of the area you intend to reserve for gardening. The map need not be complicated but should indicate the presence of natural windbreaks; existing trees; the direction of your worst winter wind; obstructions to sunlight; the house, garage, and all structures planned for the future.

First decide just how much lawn and garden you wish to care for: Nothing looks more dismal than an abandoned garden site that is overwhelmed by weeds and waits for ministrations that will never appear!

Checking the areas with natural and artificial windbreaks is very important. You might find that your future garden is in climate zone 5 where winter can chill to −20°F., but by utilizing that secluded spot next to the garage, your wind is cut in half and plants from zones 6 and 7 just might survive.

Lay out an area in full sun for a small vegetable garden, but avoid heavy traffic areas where children and pets might congregate.

If you live in an area where septic tanks are in use, remember that the soil above the tank and incoming pipes never really freezes to any great depth and thus provides a fine place for the rarer spring bulbs that resent too much cold. If you ever have to dig up the tank, the bulbs are easily gathered and moved.

Provide for the ultimate growth of any trees or bushes that you plan to grow. In ten years amazing things can happen to even

STAPELIADS IN BLOOM
The Stapeliads pictured are strange flowers indeed. Clockwise from the top right are: *Stapelia longipes, S. cylista, Edithcolea grandis, S. variegata,* **and** *S. nobilis.*

slow-growing specimens. In the meantime, empty spaces between young bushes and trees can be filled with annuals and perennials until larger plants need the room.

THE PREGNANT ONION

This is another one of those houseplants that always gets a comment from anyone who passes by. It's called the "false sea onion," the "healing onion," or, perhaps more to the point, the "pregnant onion."

The Latin name is *Ornithogalum caudatum;* the first common name refers to the plant's resemblance to another plant entirely, the sea squill *(Urginea maritima);* the second to the alleged practice of using the crushed leaves as a cauterizer over cuts and bruises, and cooked in a syrup for colds; and the third to the tiny bulbs that swell over the mother bulb's surface, growing larger until they fall to earth and become new plants.

The parent bulb is set with most of its girth above a standard soil mix, where it produces long, curved, straplike leaves that fall over the pot's edge. If given good light, a temperature of 50°F. up to 65°F., and the plant watered only after the soil has dried out, a long flowering stalk will appear—often two feet—covered with fifty or more small white flowers.

The pregnant feature of the plant is perhaps its most noticeable asset, as evidenced by the bulblets as the drawing shows. Don't remove them until they are free of the parent bulb's membrane and held by only a literal thread.

When placed on warm soil and given good light, the bulblets will start to form new plants.

THE MANGO

Almost everyone has grown an avocado in his day, but have you ever thought of starting a mango tree? With today's supersonic delivery systems, fresh mangoes are often found at the local supermarket—and you could always ask a Florida friend to send a pit up north.

The original home of the mango *(Mangifera indica)* is believed to be somewhere in eastern Asia, where it's been under cultivation for over 4,000 years. Between A.D. 632 and A.D. 640, a Chinese traveler, Hwen T'sang, brought the tree to the outside world; and by the 1700s, mangoes were grown under glass by most of the nobility of Europe. The following passage is quoted from *Curtis's Botanical Magazine* in 1850:

> The mango is recorded as having been grown in the hot-houses of this country at least 160 years ago but it is only within the last 20 years that it has come to the notice as a fruit capable of being brought to perfection in England. The first and we believe the most successful attempt was made by the Earl of Powis in his garden at Walcot where he had a lofty hot-house 400 feet long and between 30 and 40 feet wide constructed for the cultivation of the mango.

THE PREGNANT ONION
Pictured at right is one of the more conversation provoking items in the gardener's collection, the pregnant onion.

Obviously our local mangoes—at least in the colder areas—will not be grown for the fruit but merely as fascinating houseplants. The seeds (or pits) are rather perishable and will not tolerate much drying. Seeds kept at temperatures lower than 50°F. do not germinate at all well, so don't attempt it if the fruit has been refrigerated for long periods of time.

Wash the pit well of pulp, and plant not more than one inch deep in sterile soil or a typical grow-mix medium. Put it in a warm place (the warmer the better), trying to maintain at least 70°F. My plant germinated in a compost heap during the month of October where temperatures of 120°F. are normal.

When seedlings are six inches tall, transplant to a six-inch pot using a mix of soil, sand, and composted manure in quantities of one-third each. Plenty of water should be supplied during the summer months, but let the soil dry out between waterings from October to March.

As the tree grows, pot on to larger pots. You'll find that the mango plant is more attractive in form than the avocado and the leaves do not brown as easily.

In about three years from the time of germination, you can force your tree to blossom if you provide a three-month period of dry atmosphere with plenty of light.

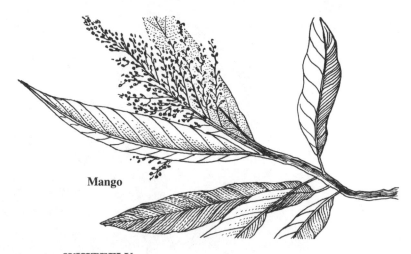

Mango

WHITEFLY

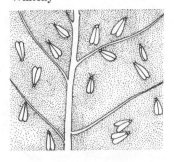

Whitefly

Plagued by whitefly? Are those spots before your eyes really those pesky little devils that fly up and about at the slightest disturbance? A few years ago, some scientists discovered that the pesky whitefly—along with a host of other insects—was attracted to the color yellow. This fact has led to the development of Sticky Strips, rigid sheets of bright yellow, about six by twelve inches and coated with glue on both sides. The flies go for the yellow and stick tight.

The strips can be either hung on strings from the ceiling or stuck on pieces of bent wire and placed directly in the pot.

They are completely safe, nontoxic, and work like a charm.

Yucca

THE PRIZED YUCCAS

Looking out of my studio window I see the barren ash trees; the leafless and small Manchurian apricot; the Persian lilac, all brown twigs—though that is full of chickadees lining up for the sunflower seeds within the hanging bird feeder; the tan and lifeless fields; various dried and shattered stems of plants long dead—in essence the landscape in late November when the snows refuse to come. Yet there is one spot of true color: fans of sharp-pointed leaves, dark green and strong, with a look more suited to Arizona deserts than New York.

These plants are the yuccas *(Yucca filamentosa),* the hardiest of the species and able to endure the northern winter without injury. Their popular name is Adam's needle since the leaves come to a needlelike point and the edges throw off numerous fine white hairs, the consistency of buttonhole thread. Most yuccas are desirable in the garden, but none is more welcome than this, especially in the North.

In the middle of summer, a strong flower stem appears, shooting up higher than the surrounding leaves—often to six feet or more—and bearing numerous cream-colored flowers, bells of bloom so thick they stand out from all else around.

In return for this bounty, the yuccas like a reasonably good soil and wish to be left alone. For once established, their long taproot makes moving a hard job. If you choose to divide a clump, try early spring and dig deep.

There is a variegated type called *Y. filamentosa* **'Bright Edge'**.

THE GRASS PALM

Every spring, garden centers across America—especially those located close to cemeteries—offer a decorative plant arrangement consisting of a few small geraniums, a sprig of ivy, and a green rosette of swordlike leaves stuck precisely in the center of the pot. The leaves are tapered, about a half-inch in width and a foot long. It's difficult to believe that this grass is really a seedling of *Cordyline australis* and will eventually become a forty-foot tree in its native New Zealand.

Nine years ago at a July clearance sale, I bought such a pot of this imaginative arrangement for 98¢. The grass caught my eye as the leaves had a leathery and permanent look. I repotted it in a five-inch pot and brought it indoors before frost. Today the trunk and leaves top seven feet standing straight and tall in a twelve-inch pot.

Use a mix of soil, sand, and compost, adding a monthly dose of plant food during the summer. Set it outdoors when weather is warm. Water well but cut back during the winter months when the tree goes into dormancy. Seeds will sprout with ease.

The one problem with the grass palm is what to do when it gets to eight feet?

Grass palm

At the beginning of winter when out driving along the coun-
tryside of the Northeast, the observant eye might spot many bright
dots of intense and shiny red that mark the site of one species of
native and northern holly, the winterberry *(Ilex verticillata).*

This small tree or shrub, with its smooth bark of warm, dull gray,
grows to a height of six to twenty feet. It's quite fond of a wettish
and swampy site, but will surprise all collectors of plant lore by
occasionally appearing on the steepest of hillsides.

Most of the year, the branches are hidden by tall field grasses,
other shrubs like sweet bush, or its larger and bushier neighbors.
The flowers are small and white, blooming in late June and early
July, escaping the notice of all but the most careful observer. They
are not the least ornamental. Not until late autumn, when most
leaves have fallen—except for the ubiquitous beech and the stately
pin oak — do the beautiful brilliant orange-red berries begin to
be seen.

Winterberry

Local birds will soon find the berries, so if you wish to cut a few
branches for effective centerpieces, start collections in early December. Keep the branches in water or the berries will shrivel and
fall off.

Winterberries are good additions to the local home landscape and
will do well in rather poor soil and even partial shade. Hardy from
zone 3 southward, they should be protected from the local deer
population until they gain a bit of stature.

Plant out in spring or fall.

A DIFFERENT SANSEVIERIA

The common mother-in-law's tongue *(Sansevieria trifasciata)*
has been found potted in every small restaurant in America, usually
in a small pot and resting on the small ledge between the steamy
window and the back edge of the booth. Sometimes they will
bloom, sending up a spike of tubular yellow flowers, sweet with
nectar, and testifying to the dignity of the plant.

There are, however, over 150 species of this plant and entire
collections of great diversity could be built of the genus. But one
stands out as stranger than the rest: *S. cylindrica,* the spear sansevieria. Leaves are rigid with a slight arch at top. This is one more
plant that visitors always ask about. They are succulent types,
preferring sandy soil, and almost seem to thrive on neglect.

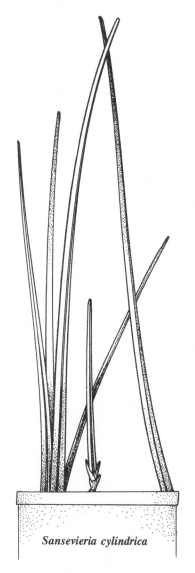

Sansevieria cylindrica

HINTS FOR NOVEMBER

Drain the pond if need be.

Turn off outdoor water taps and drain them if needed.

Redirect outdoor lighting to branches now that leaves have fallen.

Don't forget to clean the chimney if you heat with wood.

Buy potting soil, composted manure, and sand for winter work.

Put out more cages to protect trees and shrubs.

Put out feeding stations for the birds.

Once the ground is frozen, begin to apply winter mulch.

Make sure you have enough garden books for winter reading.

Make sure you mark small evergreens and shrubs so snowplows won't shear them off.

Watch the greenhouse for falling temperatures.

Apply bubble insulation to greenhouse windows.

Ready the kerosine heater.

Bring in everything left outdoors in pots.

Bring in the rest of the pots as clay will crack if wet and frozen.

NOTES

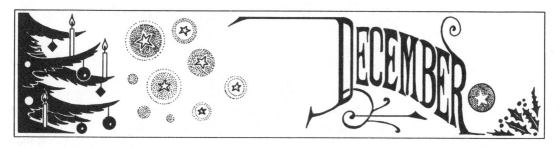

You can't forget a garden
  When you have planted seed—
When you have watched the weather
  And know a rose's need.
    LOUISE DRISCOLL

God the first garden made, and the first city, Cain.
    ABRAHAM COWLEY

A LIVING CHRISTMAS TREE

It's Christmas time and holiday time and what could be better to celebrate the end of one year, the beginning of another, than building your celebrations around a living Christmas tree?

As the years pass by, memories will be far more than broken toys and fading cards; in the yard, the reminders of pleasant times will stand fresh and green, season after season. . . .

First choose a spot for the tree, in autumn, before the ground begins to freeze. Call the nursery and discuss the type you wish to grow. The tree will be balled and burlapped, and the size of the hole you will need to dig depends on the size and kind of tree you pick. Always dig the hole a little larger than you need.

Now throw a sheet of plastic liner in the hole, put the soil back after mixing in a bit of peat moss, and cover with a layer of mulch— leaves or pine branches will be fine.

When you pick up your tree, don't put it near a radiator or any hot-air ducts in your house. Place the ball in a waterproof receptacle as the tree must be watered every day. Never allow it to dry out.

On the first good day after Christmas, take the tree outdoors and place it in the hole that you've prepared. Make a ceremony out of it. Water well, and put the soil back into place after removing the top part of the burlap bag. Mulch it well and water once again.

THE POINSETTIA

This plant means Christmas more than any other flowering plant. The colored "petals," incidentally, are really specialized leaves called "bracts"; the flowers are the tiny yellow balls that cluster in the center; the tips of the flowers produce small drops of nectar. Poinsettias *(Euphorbia pulcherrima)* are members of a large family of succulents that include the popular crown of thorns and snow-on-the-mountain; all are identified by their white, milky sap, called "latex." In tropical climates these plants assume the stature of shrubs and small trees, and if given reasonable care, they can grow to a large size even in the home.

THE POINSETTIA

The poinsettia at left shows the colorful bracts and the male flower (♂) with the female (♀). Although authorities have thought the plant very poisonous, recent investigations indicate that the cultivated strains are probably harmless but the wild plants could be bad. The sap may cause a mild dermatitis in susceptible people.

143

When you receive your plant, remove the foil wrap. The pot will be full of roots so be careful with the watering detail, wetting all the soil and not just the top. If you forget water for a day or two and the plant begins to wilt, soak it pot and all. Keep the plant in a sunny window, rotating it to maintain its full shape. Every month feed it with a liquid fertilizer. Temperatures should stay around 65°F., and try to keep plants out of direct drafts.

Continue with this treatment until the bracts start to fade, usually in late spring. When they finally go, prune the stems to below the point of flowering. The wounds might persist in bleeding latex but a quick dip in warm water (or patience) will congeal it. Repot the plant in a good all-purpose soil mix but with enough vermiculite or shredded peat moss to keep it on the light side. Move it outside as soon as weather permits. Water it well, follow the fertilizer routine, and protect it from too-hot midday sun in July and August, bringing it back indoors before the first frost threatens.

Once again it's autumn. Poinsettias are "short-day plants"—they will not set buds or go into flowering unless they have ten to twelve weeks with at least fourteen hours a day of complete darkness. And that means no light; even the glow of a streetlight or a lamp in the adjoining room will stop buds from forming. One practical solution is to put the plant in a closet every night, covered with a cardboard box or opaque plastic bag. To have flowers for Christmas, the treatment must begin the first week of October.

THE CACTUS FOR EASTER, THANKSGIVING, AND CHRISTMAS

These three cactus plants are each identified with a particular holiday as a result of their blooming habits. In nature they all grow in the crevices of tree branches, up in the air like many orchids and bromeliads, enjoying very little soil or fertilizers. In your home they need roughly the same conditions: a pot large enough to hold the shallow root systems and a mix of potting soil liberally laced with peat moss or shredded sphagnum moss plus sand or gravel. Even osmunda fibers, the growing medium for orchids, work well with these plants.

Hang the plants outdoors in the spring, in the shade of a porch or tree, and bring them inside before the first frost. During the summer, give them all feedings of liquid plant food every two weeks or so and water well.

Once back indoors, keep them in a sunny window and withhold water, keeping as close as possible to a temperature of 55–60°F.

In addition, Christmas cacti are short-day plants and will not set buds if given more than ten hours of daylight from October on. Temperatures below 50°F. are to be avoided as these chills usually halt the entire development of the plants.

The Thanksgiving, Christmas, and Easter cacti will bloom every year when given the attentions listed above.

CACTUS IN BLOOM

The three holiday cactus, showing the difference in stem structure and flowers, are pictured at the right and reading from the left: the Thanksgiving cactus *(Schumbergera truncatus)*, the Christmas cactus *(S. Bridgesii)*, and the Easter cactus *(Rhipsalidopsis Gaertneri)*.

If the flowers are hand-pollinated you will get a bonus of some extra color as plants will produce green to scarlet fruits. Transfer pollen from one flower to another using a Q-tip, brush, or fingertips. Pollen should come from another plant.

SEEDS FOR DAYS AND YEARS

Now that December is here, the seed catalogs will start to arrive and orders must be placed for next year's garden. Often at year's end we find a pile of packets—seeds that were never planted, perhaps pushed aside when we became involved with something else. Thus the following list that gives, first, the average number of days it takes for a particular type to germinate and, next, the number of years that seed is viable. Seeds should be stored in a cool, dry place.

Abutilon	20, 3–4	Eschscholtzia	5, 2
Acroclinium	15, 2–3	Euphorbia	20, 3–4
Ageratum	5, 2–3	Gaillardia	20, 2
Alyssum	5, 2–3	Geraniums	20, 3
Anchusa	20, 2	Helianthus	15, 2–4
Antirrhinum	20, 3–4	Heliotrope	15, 1
Aquilegia	15, 2	Hibiscus	15, 3–4
Asters	15, 1–2	Hollyhocks	5, 4–5
Asters, China	8, 2–3	Ipomoea	5, 3–4
Balsams	10, 6–6	Iris	50, 2
Begonias	15, 2	Kochia	15, 2
Blue Salvia	15, 2	Lantana	15, 1
Brachycome	8, 3	Larkspur	15, 3–4
Browallia	20, 2–3	Lathyrus	25, 3–4
Calendula	10, 3–4	Lobelias	8, 3–4
Candytuft	5, 2–3	Marigold	5, 3–4
Cannas	15, 3–4	Marvel of Peru	5, 2–3
Carnations	8, 3–4	Mimosa	8, 2–3
Celosia	20, 4–5	Mimulus	8, 3–4
Centaurea	5, 2	Nasturtium	8, 3–4
Chrysanthemums	5, 3–4	Nicotiana	20, 3–4
Cineraria	5, 3–4	Nigella	8, 2
Cleome	20, 2–3	Pansy	8, 2
Cobaea scandens	15, 1–2	Penstemon	20, 2
Coleus	20, 2	Petunias	20, 3–4
Coreopsis	20, 2	Platycodon	20, 2–3
Cosmos	5, 2–3	Poppies	20, 3–4
Cyperus altern.	25, 1	Portulaca	20, 3–4
Datura	15, 3–4	Salpiglossis	5, 4–5
Delphinium	15, 2	Scabiosa	20, 2–3
Dianthus	5, 3–4	Stocks	5, 4–5
Dolichos	15, 3–4	Wallflower	5, 5–6
Echinocystis	30, 4–5	Zinnias	5, 3–4

CARE OF OTHER CHRISTMAS PLANTS

Amaryllis: See p. 15.

Azalea: These plants are evergreen hybrids that have been forced to bloom for winter and spring holidays by the florist. When you receive the plant, put it in a cool spot with good, bright light; winter sun will shorten flower life but will not hurt the plant. Azaleas will endure heated rooms but should be removed every night to an area where temperatures do not exceed 65°F. Keep the soil evenly moist as these plants have very fine and wiry roots. Remove faded blossoms. Later in the spring, when all chance of frost is over, summer these plants outside in a sheltered spot and fertilize once a month with an acid-type plant food like Miracid®, continuing on into the fall. Then cut back on water—but don't allow the soil to dry out—and place the azalea in a cool spot of some 50°F. When buds have set, move into warmer quarters. When a plant outgrows its original pot, use a soil mix of one-half potting soil and one-half peat moss.

Cyclamen: See p. 1.

Jerusalem cherry *(Solanum Pseudocapsicum):* Another gift plant that if given proper care will go on for years, eventually forming a small bush of four feet. One word of warning: The cherries are said to be poisonous and children should be warned not to eat the fruit. Plants prefer bright windows with filtered sun and temperatures no higher than 70°F. during the day and 50°–60°F. at night. Keep soil evenly moist and use a standard mix of potting soil and sand, half and half. Put plants outside in summer with light shade at noon; fertilize every two to three weeks; and prune branches to half their length in early spring. When brought back indoors, plants need cool temperatures of 50°F. for about two weeks to aid in forming buds.

Kalanchoe *(Kalanchoe Blossfeldiana* **'Compacta'**): This plant is a succulent like the jade plant, coming from sunny climates and adjusting well to the dry heat of most homes. Fertilize once a month when the plant is in growth, and give about four hours of sun if you can, with summers outside. Temperatures should be about 60°–65°F. These are short-day plants like poinsettias and Christmas cacti and should get the same treatment.

CHRISTMAS WREATHS

On page 47 are instructions for making a willow or grapevine wreath for spring. Using this wreath as a base, many more elegant decorations can be had for the Christmas holidays.

Clematis blooms, after they go to seed in the fall, make marvelous white flowers when sprayed with clear lacquer to keep the plumes from breaking.

The dried flower heads of *Sedum spectabile* **'Autumn Joy'** are especially attractive on a wreath.

And don't forget combinations of white pine cones, eucalyptus sprays, rose hips (lacquer the tiny fruits), and honesty flowers *(Lunaria annua),* all attractive when affixed to the grapevines.

A walk through country fields before the bad weather truly starts will yield armloads of dried leaves, stems, and blossoms for winter decorations.

CHRISTMAS FOR THE OLD AND YOUNG

In addition to the books in the list of suggested readings, membership in any of the societies or organizations in appendix 2, and subscriptions to garden magazines, one of the items on the preceding—following page could make a fine present for a gardener.

(1) The Easi-Kneeler stool lets a gardener kneel or sit without touching the damp ground and gives them something to grip for getting back on their feet. It, (2) the Magic Handle, and (3) the Automatic Digger are all wonderful gifts for either the elderly or

the gardener afflicted with arthritis. (4) The pH Computer gives the degree of acidity or alkalinity for any soil—even in pots—without batteries. (5) The Long-Reach Limbing Saw is perfect for cutting branches up to ten feet in the air — more if you're taller. (6) The Garden Mulcher takes newspaper, which is harmless wood pulp and black carbon ink, and shreds it for mulching, the compost heap, or even animal litter. (Don't use colored sections; they have poisonous chemicals.) (7) The English-thatched Birdhouse is a decorative and functional item for the garden, and birds love it for nesting. (8) The Rattan Basket is expensive but will last a lifetime and make every trip to the garden one of style. (9) The Gardener's Belt is so useful that one wonders how we got along without it before it appeared on the scene. (10) Finally, one of the Haws Watering Cans made of high-impact red polyethylene, and the brass rose that accompanies it, would be welcomed by any plant lover.

WINTER CARE FOR PLANTS

A number of things contribute to the dull light in homes, especially during the winter months. Now that more people are burning wood for heat, a thin film builds up on windows: The result is less light. We often keep shades drawn even during the day to conserve heat: thus less light. Plastic storm windows do their share, and cloudy days wind up the battle.

You can get an idea of light intensity with a regular camera by using the exposure meter to measure foot candles (FC) — the amount of light cast on a white surface by one candle, one foot away, in an otherwise dark room. Set the film speed to ASA 200, the shutter speed to 1/500th second, and

f22 = 5,000 FC	f8 = 550 FC
f16 = 2,500 FC	f6.3 = 300 FC
f11 = 1,200 FC	f4.5 = 150 FC

Plants that need full sun, such as most cacti and flowering annuals, generally require 6,000 to 8,000 FC. Ferns, most begonias, and many jungle-born houseplants prefer partial shade or an average of 2,000 FC. Deep-jungle dwellers like 250 to 500 FC.

Many plants will survive in 20 FC for a short time, but 100 FC seems to be the minimum needed for growth and sustaining life.

Windows immediately cut down on light intensity through outside refraction by the glass and the fact that some light is actually absorbed by the glass itself. Such architectural details as eaves and cornices mean the loss of more light: A west window in midmorning may read 400 FC at the inside sill, but only 10 FC when measured from six feet into the room, while outdoors the light will be 10,000 FC. A thin layer of dust on the tops of leaves further cuts down the amount of light that's received by most houseplants. Plants should be dusted and cleaned right along with books and tabletops. While 50 FC is a comfortable light for reading a newspaper, it's hardly enough to keep a plant alive, much less healthy.

GIFTS FOR CHRISTMAS
Pictured at left are some of the gifts that gardeners would love to receive for the holidays.

INCIDENTAL INTELLIGENCE

After dirt, labor, and plants, nothing is more important to a garden than good tools. Like most else in life, it pays to buy the best you can afford.

Good tools are made of forged metal, formed by the manufacturer by banging hot metal into the desired shape with hammers and presses. It takes muscle, both machine and human, and the resulting tools are durable and heavy.

Less-expensive tools are made of rolled steel that is cut in the desired shape in the same way a cook cuts a cookie with a cutter. You wind up with a tool that will easily bend under pressure.

Look at the place where the handle meets the metal tool. Is it held by screws and/or rivets? If just held by force, chances are the handle will eventually work loose—just when you need it the most.

Clean all your garden tools before storing them for the winter. Keep a wooden spatula hanging in a handy place to help in scraping packed and dried soil clods from hoes, shovels, and other diggers. Keep a sharpening stone handy so that all cutting edges are ready to cut.

Up north, drain the lawn mower, cultivator, and other power tools of gasoline. Like everything else, gasoline gets old, eventually becoming gummy and refusing to ignite.

HERBS FOR KEEPING

I hate to mention it, as I'm one of those people who have spoken against microwave ovens for years—I won't have one in the house —but garden friends who have these monsters have informed me that nothing beats electronic marvels for drying herbs. Wash, drain, and remove the major stems from gathered herbs. Then dry them in the microwave, winding up by rubbing through a wire strainer to break up larger pieces, and bottle immediately.

VARIEGATIONS FOR VARIETY

The four houseplants pictured at right are all old favorites but liven up a typical green outlook by sporting various shades of white. Clockwise from top right are the cast-iron plant *(Aspidistra elatior* 'Variegata'); the screw pine *(Pandanus Veitchii);* the clown fig *(Ficus aspera);* and the large spider plant *(Chlorophytum comosum variegatum).*

They all prefer temperatures above 50°F.; in fact the clown fig will drop its leaves in protest when the thermometer falls below that mark—it will recover when warmed up.

A soil mix of one-half good potting soil, one-quarter sharp sand, and one-quarter composted manure is fine for all.

THE GARDENIA

A few flakes of light snow are falling on this last night of the year. They will not last, for temperatures are too high and the thin clouds above are quickly blowing away. Though it's December, the landscape is still barren, fields and woods of brown, not white.

Yet in my study, one small white gardienia has opened, its perfume filling the room with thoughts of tropical nights and gentle winds. It was a gift from a charming lady who lives down the road.

She had cared for this plant over many years. It began as a small houseplant purchased at a local supermarket, but has grown into a shrub four feet in diameter and four feet high, inhabiting a twelve-inch tub.

Requirements for this gardenia *(Gardenia jasminoides* var. *Fortuniana)* are not taxing, except for a need of warmth—60°F. and up. It will survive 52°F. without damage, but is clear in its dislike, for leaves slowly drop or yellow. Strangely for a tropical plant, temperatures of 58–60°F. are needed for bud formation.

Give gardenias sunny windows in winter, and summers on the patio.

Every three weeks of active growth or flowering, a plant food is administered. Potting soil is fine but should be cut with one-half peat moss: Gardenias like an acid medium for growth.

Keep the soil moist as roots are thin and fragile, drying quickly without adequate water.

There are more buds waiting in the wings.... I foresee a winter of blossoms and a plant that will be well remembered over the years.

Gardenia

HINTS FOR DECEMBER

Be careful of mice in the greenhouse.

Plant paper-whites and lilies of the valley in stone chips.

Mulch the rock garden, if so inclined, but only if the ground is frozen. I put chicken wire over white pine boughs to keep rabbits and deer at bay.

Don't overwater succulents and cacti.

Drop hints to friends for garden gifts.

Watch for falling temperatures in the greenhouse.

Keep incoming catalogs together for a good read as snow flies and wind blows.

NOTES

APPENDIXES

Appendix 1:

Magazines and Newsletters

The following publications are available by subscription in the United States including two that are published in England. I have noted those that include membership in separate seed exchanges.

American Horticulturist publishes six magazines and six newsletters per year at a cost of $20 and is part of membership in the American Horticultural Society. The magazine is one of the best around for both the serious gardener and the amateur, with an emphasis on flowers. Production and illustrations are excellent. (Also listed in appendix 2.)
—American Horticultural Society, Mount Vernon, Virginia 22121.

The Avant Gardener is a monthly newsletter costing $15 per year and dealing with all aspects of horticulture. It's for the serious amateur and professional, and covers news items and developments in horticulture and related subjects.
—Box 489, New York, New York 10028.

Flower and Garden is a bimonthly magazine that's been a friend to gardeners for years. It covers both flowers and vegetables in a newsy, how-to-manner. Price: $6 per year.
—4251 Pennsylvania Ave., Kansas City, Missouri 64111.

Garden is a bimonthly magazine published by the New York Botanical Garden for $10 per year. It is free with membership in the society and covers all aspects of gardening.
—New York Botanical Garden, Bronx, New York 10458.

The Garden is a monthly magazine published by the Royal Horticultural Society of England. It is only one feature of a membership (see p. 158). From garden design to the newest in both indoor and outdoor plants, it has something for everyone. The cost is $18 per year, but exchange rates vary.
—Vincent Square, London SW 1P 2PE, England.

Garden Design is a new quarterly published by the ·American Society of Landscape Architects. It presents fine photos and plans of all kinds of garden design both here and abroad, and costs $15 per year.
—1190 E. Broadway, Louisville, Kentucky 40204.

Gardens for All is a monthly news magazine that deals with all aspects of the garden but leans toward vegetables and how-to projects. Price: $12 per year.
—180 Flynn Ave., Burlington, Vermont 05401.

Green Scene appears on a bimonthly schedule with fine articles on gardening, indoors and out. One wishes for more. While dealing with the Delaware Valley, most of the information is good through-

out the country. Price $8.50 per year.
—325 Walnut St., Philadelphia, Pennsylvania 19106.

The Herb Quarterly is a well-produced and very interesting quarterly devoted entirely to herbs and their cultivation for $15 per year.
—Newfane, Vermont 05345.

Horticulture is a monthly covering all aspects of gardening and is one of the most elegant productions on the market. Price: $18 per year.
—300 Massachusetts Ave., Boston, Massachusetts 02115.

Pacific Horticulture is a quarterly out of California but always has something of interest to all gardeners in the country. Illustrations are excellent and articles scholarly. Price: $10 per year.
—P.O. Box 485, Berkeley, California 94701.

Plants and Gardens is a quarterly published by the Brooklyn Botanical Garden and covers a different theme of gardening with each issue, always well done. Price: $10 per year.
—1000 Washington Ave., Brooklyn, New York 11225.

The Plantsman is a quarterly from England and, while very scientific in its outlook, it has much information of value for the serious gardener. The price is $18 per year, but the exchange rate will vary.
—Artists House, 14-15 Manette St., London W1V 5LB, England.

In addition to the above, there are many decorating magazines on the market. Most, like *House & Garden,* have garden sections and columns; a few, as *Architectural Digest,* feature well-known gardens, and many important newspapers have garden columns.

Appendix 2:

Organizations that Publish Bulletins and/or Sponsor Seed Exchanges

The following organizations all have publications and/or seed exchanges of great diversity. Most are overseas, but do not let that stop you from joining: The mails go through, albeit slowly.

Alpine Garden Society is mainly concerned with alpine and rock-garden plants. Its quarterly bulletin is stocked with valuable information; the seed exchange is annual and lists well over 4,000 varieties. Both are available to members for $15 per year.
—Lye End Link, St. John's Woking GU21 1SW, Surrey, England.

American Horticultural Society, in addition to its magazine p. 156, sponsors a seed exchange for members. The seed exchange is included in the $20 membership fee.
—Mount Vernon, Virginia 22121.

American Rock Garden Society publishes a fine quarterly bulletin and sponsors the biggest seed exchange in the United States and Canada. Over 3,500 different types are offered as part of membership. Cost is $9 per year.
—Donald M. Peach, Secretary, Rte. 1, Box 282, Mena, Arkansas 71953.

Hardy Plant Society is a fine old English organization that publishes various news bulletins and one annual bulletin, and sponsors a fine and select seed exchange. Cost is $8 per year.
—Hon. Sec. Miss Barbara White, 10 St. Barnabas Road, Emmer Green, Cabersham, Reading RG4 8RA, England.

Japanese Rock Garden Society has recently opened its doors to worldwide membership. The yearly journal is in both Japanese and English and the seed exchange is fascinating. Cost is $15 per year and an International Postal Money Order is needed.
—Noriyoshi Masuda, 943-123 Nibuno, Himeji, Japan.

Royal Horticultural Society is one of the all-time greats. In addition to *The Garden,* the monthly magazine (see p. 156), membership includes a free pass to the Chelsea Flower Show, and the seed exchange that covers the world with 1,200 entries. Cost is about $20 per year.
—Vincent Square, London SW1P 2PE, England.

Scottish Rock Garden Society publishes two fine bulletins per year and sponsors a seed exchange of surprising complexity with 3,200 entries. Membership is $12 per year.
—Mrs. E.R. Law, Kippielaw Farm, by Haddington, East Lothian EH41 4 PY, Scotland.

The following two seed exchanges do not easily fall into any other categories so are listed here.

Alpina Research keeps a seed bank and maintains an annual seed-exchange list of unusual varieties.
—630 S.E. Rene, Gresham, Oregon 97030.

Major Howell's International Seed Collection stocks hundreds of varieties of seed from all types of botanical collections throughout the world. Membership and lists are $10 per year, including first six seed choices.
—Fire Thorn, 6 Oxshott Way, Cobham, Surrey, KT11 2RT, England.

Appendix 3:

Plant Societies

The following plant societies are dedicated to the pursuit of special interests as their names imply. Membership usually includes special publications, seed exchanges, and invitations to regional meetings.

African Violet Society—P.O. Box 1326, Knoxville, Tennessee 37901

American Bamboo Society—1101 San Leon Ct., Solana Beach, California 92075

American Begonia Society—369 Ridge Vista Ave., San Jose, California 95127

American Bonsai Society—Box 358, Keene, New Hampshire 03431

American Boxwood Society—Box 85, Boyce, Virginia 22620

American Camellia Society—Box 1217, Fort Valley, Georgia 31030

American Daffodil Society—Tyner, North Carolina 27980

American Dahlia Society—1649 Beech, Melrose Park, Pennsylvania 19126

American Fern Society—George Mason University, Fairfax, Virginia 22030

American Fuchsia Society—Hall of Flowers, Golden Gate Park, San Francisco, California 94122

American Gloxinia Society—Box 312, Ayer, Massachusetts 01432

American Hemerocallis Society—Route 2, Box 360, DeQueen, Arkansas 71832

American Hibiscus Society—206 N.E. 40th St., Pompano Beach, Florida 33064

American Hosta Society—5605 11th Avenue South, Birmingham, Alabama 35222

American Iris Society—2315 Tower Grove Ave., St. Louis, Missouri 63110

American Ivy Society—National Center for American Horticulture, Mount Vernon, Virginia 22121

American Magnolia Society—14876 Pheasant Hill Court, Chesterfield, Missouri 63017

American Orchid Society—Botanical Museum of Harvard University, Cambridge, Massachusetts 02138

American Penstemon Society—Cox Arboretum, 6733 Springboro Pike, Dayton, Ohio 45449

American Peony Society—250 Interlachen Rd., Hopkins, Minnesota 55343

American Primrose Society—Grout Hill, South Acworth, New Hampshire 03607

American Rhododendron Society—617 Fairway Dr., Aberdeen, Washington 98520

American Rose Society—Box 30,000, Shreveport, Louisiana 71130

Bromeliad Society—P.O. Box 41261, Los Angeles, California 90041

Cactus and Succulent Society of America—Box 3010, Santa Barbara, California 93105

Carniverous Plant Society— % Mrs. Pat Hansen, The Fullerton Arboretum, Department of Biology, California State University, Fullerton, California 92634

Cymbidium Society of America—469 W. Norman Ave., Arcadia, California 91006

Dwarf Conifer Notes—Theophrastus, P.O. Box 458, Little Compton, Rhode Island 02837

Epiphyllum Society of America—P.O. Box 1395, Monrovia, California 91016

Holly Society of America—407 Fountain Green Rd., Bel Air, Maryland 21014

Indoor Light Gardening Society of America—RD 5, Box 76, East Stroudsburg, Pennsylvania 18301

International Asclepiad Society—Mrs. J. Gutteridge, 3 Annes Walk, Caterham, Surrey, CR3 5EL, England

International Cactus and Succulent Society—P.O. Box 253, Odessa, Texas 79760

International Geranium Society—6501 Yosemite Dr., Dept. 7, Buena Park, California 90620

National Chrysanthemum Society—2612 Beverly Blvd. S.W., Roanoke, Virginia 24014

North American Gladiolus Council—30 Highland Place, Peru, Indiana 48970

North American Lily Society—Box 40134, Indianapolis, Indiana 46240

The Palm Society—P.O. Box 368, Lawrence, Kansas 66044

Sempervivum Fanciers Association—37 Ox Bow Lane, Randolph, Massachusetts

Appendix 4:

Commercial Seed Companies

The following list consists of catalogs issued by seed companies only. Because of fluctuating costs, I've not included any charges involved with receiving these publications, so write first.

This list is in no way a complete count of seed companies in business today.

Abundant Life Seed Foundation—P.O. Box 772, Port Townsend, Washington 98368. Dedicated to keeping species from disappearing from the scene.

Applewood Seed Company—5380 Viviar St., Arvada, Colorado 80002. Wildflower seeds.

The Banana Tree—715 Northampton St., Easton, Pennsylvania 18042. Exotic seeds; bananas, trees, flowers.

Burpee Gardens—Warminster, Pennsylvania 18974. A major seed company.

Chiltern Seeds—Bortree Stile, Ulverston, Cumbria LA12 7PB England. One of the biggest in the world with a fascinating catalog.

Comstock, Ferre & Co.—A most complete collection from an old and established company.

The Cotton Boll—P.O. Box 156, Hayneville, Alabama 36040. More odd seeds.

William Dam Seeds—P.O. Box 8400, Dundas, Ontario, Canada L9H 6M1. One of Canada's oldest and finest firms.

DeGiorgi Company, Inc.—Council Bluffs, Iowa 51502. Seventy-eight years of selling seeds in America.

J.A. Demonchaux Company—827 N. Kansas, Topeka, Kansas 66608. Very fancy seeds and foods from France.

Jack Drake—Aviemore, Inverness-shire, Scotland PH22 1QS. Rare flower seeds for the rock garden.

Epicure Seeds—Box 23568, Rochester, New York 14692. Fancy vegetable seeds from all over the world.

Exotica Seed Co.—8033 Sunset Blvd., Suite 125, West Hollywood, California 90046. Exotics from all over the world.

Exotic Tropical Seeds: KEO Entities—348 Chelsea Circle, Land o'Lakes, Florida 33539. Another importer of fanciful seeds.

Far North Gardens—16785 Harrison, Livonia, Michigan 48154. A wonderful collection of seeds both domestic and wild.

G. Seed Company—Box 95, Rutherford, California 94573. One of the many small seed companies sprouting up in America with specialized collections.

Gleckeler's Seedsmen—Metamora, Ohio 43540. Giant marigolds, their specialty.

L.S.A. Goodwin & Sons—Goodwins Road, Bagdad, Sth-7407 Tasmania. Yes, specialized seeds from Tasmania. Worth writing for.

Jonathan Green's Seed Catalog—Box 9, Farmingdale, New Jersey 07727. Many types of seeds from England.

Guerney's Seed & Nursery Co.—Yankton, South Dakota 57079. An old-fashioned catalog with old-fashioned pictures of flowers and vegetables.

Hana Gardenland—P.O. Box 248, Hana, Maui, Hawaii 96713. Plants and seeds from Hawaii.

Herbst Seed Company—1000 N. Main St., Brewster, New York 10509. A famous old firm with a fine collection of diverse seeds.

M. Holtzhausen Seeds—14 High Cross St., St. Austell, Cornwall, England. Another worthwhile catalog full of interesting items.

Horticultural Enterprises—P.O. Box 340082, Dallas, Texas 75234. Wild plants and the world's most complete selection of hot peppers.

J.L. Hudson, Seedsman—P.O. Box 1058, Redwood City, California 94064. A giant selection of interesting seeds from all over.

Johnny's Selected Seeds—Albion, Maine 04910. Mostly vegetables, but a fine line of herb seeds.

Jung Quality Seeds—Randolph, Wisconsin 53956. Another American great with a complete line of choices.

LaFayette Home Nursery, Inc.—Lafayette, Illinois 61449. Seeds of prairie plants and native grasses.

Earl May Seed & Nursery—Shenandoah, Iowa 51603. One more famous American nursery with a large selection.

The Naturalists—P.O. Box 435, Yorktown Heights, New York 10598. Wild herb and flower seeds of all types.

Nichol's Herb and Rare Seeds—1190 N. Pacific Highway, Albany, Oregon 97321. Large collection of special seeds: herbs, flowers, bulbs.

Olds Seed Co.—P.O. Box 7790, 2901 Packers Ave., Madison, Wisconsin 53707. Annuals, perennials, flowers for all.

Park Seed Co.—Greenwood, South Carolina 29647. One of the most famous in America, with many choices.

Steve Pirus—P.O. Box 693, Westminster, California 92683. Rare and exotic seeds.

Plants of the Southwest—1570 Pacheco St., Santa Fe, New Mexico 87501. An interesting catalog with many wildflowers and grasses.

Clyde Robin Seed Catalog—P.O. Box 2855, Castro Valley, California 94546. One of the first major dealers in wildflower seeds.

Rocky Mountain Seed Company—Box 215, Golden B.C., Canada V0A 1H0. Many interesting seeds from the far North.

R.H. Shumway—Rockford, Illinois 61101. Another American institution where seeds are concerned.

Stokes Seed Company—Box 548, Buffalo, New York 14240. An attractive catalog with many flower offerings.

Thompson & Morgan—P.O. Box 100, Farmingdale, New Jersey 07727. One of England's oldest seed houses, now with offices in America.

Otis Twilley Seed Co.—P.O. Box 65, Trevose, Pennsylvania 19047. Select flower and vegetable hybrids.

Appendix 5:

Live Plants by Mail

The following suppliers grow and sell live plants as opposed to seeds. Over the years I've ordered hundreds of plants by mail from places as far off as London. Through the auspices of the United Parcel Service, most everything has arrived in good to fine shape. The firms listed below have learned through experience how to wrap and ship live plants — and they are eminently fair people, ready to hear from you, the buyer, if you have a problem.

The following list puts me on the line as I've dealt with them all. Addresses are up-to-date as of spring, 1983. There is a catalog fee listed where practical to do so. If in doubt, write.

Alpenglow—13328 King George Highway, Surrey, B.C., Canada V3T 2T6. The catalog is $1 and lists many fine and unusual hardy alpines, perennials, and shrubs for the garden.

Altman Specialty Plants — 553 Buena Creek Rd., San Marcos, California 92069. The catalog is $1 and includes a large variety of unusual succulent plants from all over the world.

Kurt Bluemel, Inc. — 2543 Hess Rd., Fallston, Maryland 21047. The catalog costs 50¢ and includes the largest selection of ornamental grasses available in the country. Includes sedges and rushes.

The Bovees Nursery — 1737 S.W. Coronado, Portland, Oregon 97219. The catalog is $1 and features rhododendrons, azaleas, and a large number of companion plants for the evergreen garden.

Coenosium Gardens—425 N. Fifth St., Lehighton, Pennsylvania 18235. A fascinating collection of dwarf conifers. Send self-addressed and stamped envelope (SASE) for the list.

Country Hills Greenhouse—RR#2, Corning, Ohio 43720. Send $2.50 for one of the largest and most complete catalogs covering a fantastic collection of houseplants, both common and extremely rare.

C.A. Cruickshank Ltd. — 1015 Mount Pleasant Rd., Toronto, Ontario M4P 2M1, Canada. A complete selection of garden bulbs, perennials, and many gladiolus. Catalog is $1.

The Cummins Garden — 22 Robertsville Rd., Marlboro, New Jersey 07746. Catalog is $1 and includes a fine selection of dwarf and small evergreens along with companion plants.

Endangered Species—12571 Red Hill Avenue, Tustin, California 92680. The complete catalog costs $4 and includes a number of newsletters and special price lists of unusual plants along with the *magnum opus*. The selection of both indoor and outdoor plants is staggering.

Far North Gardens—16785 Harrison, Livonia, Michigan 48154. The catalog is $1 and they are listed here because of the fine collection of hard-to-find primroses they offer by mail.

Flintridge Herb Farm — Rte. 1, Box 187, Sister Bay, Wisconsin 54234. A very large selection of herbs is offered. Catalog is $1.

Garden Place — 6780 Heisley Rd., P.O. Box 83, Mentor, Ohio 44060. A good all-around selection of hardy garden perennials from *Achillea* to *Yucca*. Catalog is 50¢.

Gardens of the Blue Ridge—P.O. Box 10, Pineola, North Carolina 28662. A number of wildflower perennials along with shrubs, ferns, and vines.

Girard Nurseries — P.O. Box 428, Geneva, Ohio 44041. A fine selection of small evergreens and hollies.

Greer Gardens—1280 Goodpasture Island Rd., Eugene, Oregon 97401. The catalog costs $2 and offers a bewildering selection of rhododendrons, azaleas, and a good choice of maple cultivars.

Holbrook Farm — Rte. 2, Box 223 B, Fletcher, North Carolina 28732. Catalog is $1 and includes a number of interesting native American wildflowers and bulbs for naturalizing. Two catalogs per year, spring and fall.

Hortica Gardens — P.O. Box 308, Placerville, California 95667. The catalog is 50¢. Listings include a number of plants suitable for bonsai training and small evergreens.

International Growers Exchange — Box 397, Farmington, Michigan 48024. Catalogs cost $3 and include the general catalog, spring and fall; the wholesale price list (which includes a retail section); and the latest sale lists of imported and domestic bulbs. This place is a true potpourri of plants.

Lamb Nurseries — E. 101 Sharp Ave., Spokane, Washington 99202. The catalog is $1. Listings include hardy perennials, alpines, and many garden mums.

Las Pilitas Nursery — Star Rte., Box 23x, Santa Margarita, California 93453. The catalog is $1 and features native plants of California, many of them hardy to −20°F., thus running the zonal gambit from 10 to 5.

Logee's Greenhouses—Danielson, Connecticut 06239. Catalog is $2.50 and includes a vast number of geraniums, flowering maples, and exotic houseplants from around the world.

John D. Lyon, Inc. — 143 Alewife Brook Parkway, Cambridge, Massachusetts 02140. Send a SASE for the list of many unusual bulbs for naturalizing, both in the perennial border and the rock garden.

Milaeger's Gardens — 4838 Douglas Ave., Racine, Wisconsin 53402. The catalog is $1 and includes a fine listing of hardy perennials for the garden. A few garden plans are pictured in the catalog.

Miniature Roses Company—200 Rose Ridge, Greenwood, South Carolina 29647. Catalog is free and includes many of the more popular miniature roses.

Oliver Nurseries, Inc.—1159 Bronson Rd., Fairfield, Connecticut 06430. Oliver's does not ship, but the nursery includes such a perfect collection of fine pines and rock garden evergreens that they are included here if you live close enough for a trip to their gardens.

Orchid Gardens—6700 Splithand Rd., Grand Rapids, Minnesota 55744. The catalog is 50¢ and is dedicated to wildflowers, hardy ferns, and some perennials.

Pellett Garden — Atlantic, Iowa 50022. Send a SASE for the catalog, which deals entirely with plants popular with bees.

Peter Pauls Nurseries—Canandaigua, New York 14424. Send a SASE for the plant listings at this the biggest dealer in carnivorous plants. The selection is very large.

Powell's Gardens — Rte. 2, Highway 70, Princeton, North Carolina 27569. The catalog is $1.50 and covers many day lilies, hostas, and hardy perennials for the border.

Rakestraw's Perennial Gardens—G-3094 S. Term St., Burton, Michigan 48529. The catalog is $1 and lists many sedums, perennials, and dwarf conifers.

Rocknoll Nursery — 9210 U.S. 50, Hillsboro, Ohio 45133. The catalog is 40¢ in stamps and features a very personal collection of rock-garden alpines and perennials gathered over a lifetime. Good selection of coralbells.

Roses of Yesterday and Today — Brown's Valley Rd., Watsonville, California 95076. The catalog is $1 and a must for the rose lovers among us.

Sandy Mush Herbs—Rte. 2, Surrett Cove Rd., Leicester, North Carolina 28748. The catalog is $1 and includes a diverse selection of herbs and garden perennials, especially thymes.

David B. Sindt-Irises—1331 W. Cornelia, Chicago, Illinois 60657. Send a 20¢ stamp for this catalog, which deals with the most complete collection of irises available today.

Siskiyou Rare Plant Nursery — 2825 Cummings Rd., Medford, Oregon 97501. Catalog is $1.50 and is a marvelous collection of the best in rock-garden plants, including ferns, and many unusual items.

Louis Smirnow — 85 Linden Lane, Glen Head P.O., Brookville, Long Island, New York 11545. Catalog is $1 and features tree peonies, both large and small, plus herbaceous peonies and species types.

Starmont Daylilies — 16415 Shady Grove Road, Gaithersburg, Maryland 20760. Catalog is 50¢ and contains listings for hundreds of day lilies.

Stonecrop Nurseries — Cold Spring, New York 10516. Send a SASE for a listing of the unusual rock-garden plants and perennials offered by this nursery on the Hudson River.

Sweet Springs Perennial Growers—2065 Ferndale Rd., Arroyo Grande, California 93420. A large selection of garden perennials for those living on the West Coast. Catalog is $1.

Dr. Warren Stoutamire—3615 Mogadore Rd., Mogadore, Ohio 44260. Dr. Stoutamire is the only source in the U.S. — to my knowledge—for the disa orchids.

Thompson's Begonias—P.O. Drawer PP, Southampton, New York 11968. Catalog is $1 for the world's most complete listing of begonias.

William Tricker, Inc.—74 Allendale Ave., P.O. Box 398, Saddle River, New Jersey 07458. Catalog is $1 and covers all types of plants and materials for the water garden, including water lilies, and fish.

Andre Viette Farm & Nursery — Rte. 1, Box 16, Fishersville, Virginia 22939. Catalog is $1 and includes many fine day lilies, hostas, ornamental grasses, and garden irises.

Wayside Gardens—Hodges, South Carolina 29695. The catalog is $1 and boasts a tremendous number of color pictures of the plants, shrubs, and small trees that they offer.

White Flower Farm — Litchfield, Connecticut 06759. The catalogs are $5 per year and include spring and fall editions of *The Garden Book,* as much a guide to the garden as a listing of plants offered.

Winterthur's Plant Shop—The Plant Shop, Winterthur Museum and Gardens, Winterthur, Delaware 19735. Send $1 for the price list of many rare and unusual plants grown at the Winterthur Museum.

Woodlanders—1128 Colleton Ave., Aiken, South Carolina 29801. Send $2 for a descriptive catalog and price list for many fine wildflowers and plants.

In addition to all of the above, the Mailorder Association of Nurseymen has prepared a guidebook that lists major by-mail sources for hundreds of items, alphabetically arranged. For a free copy, send a self-addressed business-size envelope with 40¢ in stamps to: Mailorder Association of Nurserymen, Inc., 210 Cartwright Blvd., Massapequa Park, New York 11762.

Appendix 6:

Garden and Greenhouse Equipment Sources

The following firms stock tools, insulation, stoves, labels, watering equipment, and all kinds of garden and greenhouse items.

Brookstone—127 Vose Farm Rd., Peterborough, New Hampshire 03458. Hard-to-find tools, including a number of specialty items for the garden.

Charley's Greenhouse Supply—12815 N.E. 124th St., Kirkland, Washington 98033. A major supplier of greenhouse-related items, including the new bubble insulation.

Davidson's Quality Tools—P.O. Box 195, Wellesley, Massachusetts 02181. Finely made small tools and cultivators.

Erkins Sculpture Garden—14 E. 41st St., New York, New York 10017. Marvelous collection of pots and garden ornaments.

Faire Harbour Ltd.—44 Captain Peirce Rd., Scituate, Massachusetts 02066. Kerosine heaters and replacement parts for Aladdin stoves.

Gardener's Eden — 25 Huntington at Copley Square, Boston, Massachusetts 02116. A large collection of garden items.

A.M. Leonard, Inc. — 6665 Spiker Rd., Piqua, Ohio 45356. A major horticultural tool-and-supply catalog.

McKee's Houseplant Corner — P.O. Box 96, Northfield, New Jersey 08225. Many items for houseplant growers: pots, etc.

Mellinger's—2310 W. South Range Rd., North Lima, Ohio 44452. Although they stock a number of plants and seeds, they are best for being a hardware store for gardeners.

Walt Nicke—Box 667G, Hudson, New York 12534. A supermarket of all kinds of garden equipment, much from England.

Smith & Hawken Tool Company — 68 Homer, Palo Alto, California 94301. A major collection of quality garden tools and watering devices.

Appendix 7:

A Metric Conversion System

When you know:	You can find:	If you multiply by:
Inches	Millimeters	25.
Inches	Centimeters	2.5
Feet	Centimeters	30.
Centimeters	Inches	0.4
Millimeters	Inches	0.04
Degrees Celsius	Degrees Fahrenheit	1.8 and then add 32
Degrees Fahrenheit	Degrees Celsius	0.56 after subtracting 32

Appendix 8:

Hardiness Zone Chart

A word of warning: There are two hardiness zone maps at large in the United States. One is published by the Agricultural Research Service of the U.S. Department of Agriculture; the other is backed by the Arnold Arboretum of Harvard University. The two maps generate a great deal of confusion as they do *not* match!

When ordering plants from any catalog, check to see which system they are using. The temperatures for each are given below. This book uses the USDA map.

**Approximate Range of Average Annual
Minimum Temperature for each Zone**

USDA		ARNOLD ARBORETUM	
Zone 1	Below −50°F	Zone 1	Below −50°F
Zone 2	−50° to −40°	Zone 2	−35° to −50°
Zone 3	−40° to −30°	Zone 3	−20° to −35°
Zone 4	−30° to −20°	Zone 4	−10° to −20°
Zone 5	−20° to −10°	Zone 5	− 5° to −10°
Zone 6	−10° to 0°	Zone 6	− 5° to 5°
Zone 7	0° to 10°	Zone 7	5° to 10°
Zone 8	10° to 20°	Zone 8	10° to 20°
Zone 9	20° to 30°	Zone 9	20° to 30°
Zone 10	30° to 40°	Zone 10	30° to 40°

Sources

Most of the plants and products described in this book are available from the suppliers listed in the various appendixes. A few that are exclusive offerings appear below.

Japanese Lantern (p. iii): Smithsonian Institution Gift Shop, Washington, D.C. 20013.

The Sun-gro ®(p. 19): Medallion Products, Alexandria, Virginia 22308.

The Arbor (p. 28): Brookstone Company, 127 Vose Farm Road, Peterborough, New Hampshire 03458.

Outdoor Lighting (p. 45): Rainbow Bright®, Perfect-Line Division, 80 East Gates Avenue, Lindenhurst, New York 11757.

The Black Cat (p. 62): The Shop in the Garden, The New York Botanical Garden, Bronx, New York 10458.

Easy-Kneeler, Magic Handle, Automatic Digger (pp. 148-49): Gardens for All, 180 Flynn Avenue, Burlington, Vermont. **English-Thatched Birdhouse, Gardener's Belt:** Walt Nicke, Box 667G, Hudson, New York 12534. **The Rattan Basket:** White Flower Farm, Litchfield, Connecticut 06759.

Suggested Reading

Bisset, Peter. *The Book of Water Gardening.* New York: A. T. De La Mare, 1907.

A wonderful walk down memory lane to a time when water gardening was done primarily on large and grand estates; but full of ideas.

Bloom, Alan. *Alpines for Your Garden.* Chicago: Floraprint U.S.A., 1981.

Beautiful color pictures and excellent advice on starting rock gardens.

————. *Perennials for Your Garden.* Nottingham, England: Floraprint Ltd., 1971.

More fine pictures with good flower selections by a master gardener.

Britton, Nathaniel Lord, and Addison Brown. *An Illustrated Flora of the Northern United States and Canada.* 3 vols. 1913. Reprint. New York: Dover, 1970.

Covers just about everything growing in the United States; and while some botanical names have changed, the descriptions and illustrations are as good as ever.

Brooks, John. *Room Outside: A Plan for the Garden.* New York: Viking, 1970.

Covers everything you need to know about creative landscape design on small plots of land.

————*The Small Garden.* London: Marshall Cavendish, 1977.

The single best book on designing and building a small garden. A must for any garden library.

Coats, Peter. *Plants for Connoisseurs.* Indianapolis/New York: Bobbs-Merrill, 1974.

A fine picture book of gardens and plantings, many of which will grow with equal ease in America or England. Great to look at when spirits need to be brightened.

Crowe, Sylvia. *Garden Design.* London: Thomas Gibson, 1981.

Although an English book, this contains much of use to any American gardener interested in the study of design principles as related to the contemporary landscape.

Dictionary of Gardening. The Royal Horticultural Society. 4 vols. and supplement. Oxford: Clarendon, 1965.

Next to *Hortus Third,* these volumes are the most used in my library. Fascinating not only for advice in plants and planting, but history, too.

Frederick, William H., Jr. *100 Great Garden Plants.* New York: Alfred A. Knopf, 1975.

Good color pictures and a good selection of plants but best for the gardener with a bit of land. Very American in outlook.

Gault, S. Millar, and George Kalmbacher. *The Color Dictionary of Shrubs.* New York: Crown, 1976.

This, too, is an English book, but adapted to the American

climate and consisting of beautiful pictures with excellent advice on culture.

Genders, Roy. *Bulbs: A Complete Handbook.* Indianapolis/New York: Bobbs-Merrill, 1973.
A complete handbook of cultural instructions for most bulbs, corms, and tubers being grown today.

Graf, Alfred Byrd. *Exotic Plant Manual.* East Rutherford, N.J.: Roehrs, 1970.
Contains 4,200 black-and-white photos along with complete cultural tips and requirements for houseplants. A masterpiece of editing.

Harkness, Bernard E. *The Seedlist Handbook,* 2nd ed. Bellona, N.Y.: Kashong, 1976.
A listing of all the plants in the seed exchanges of the American Rock Garden Society and a valuable checklist.

Hay, Roy, and Patrick M. Synge. *Color Dictionary of Flowers and Plants.* New York: Crown, 1975.
A very valuable addition to any plant library, with hundreds of small but clear color photos of perennial and annual plants and flowers. Another well-thumbed book.

Heath, Royton E. *The Collingridge Guide to Collectors' Alpines.* Surrey, England: Collingridge, 1981.
Beautiful photos and clear instructions on the cultivation of alpine plants both in frames and alpine houses.

Hortus Third. New York: Macmillan, 1976.
This is the monumental revision of L. H. Bailey and Ethel Zöe Bailey's original work of nomenclature for the American gardener, overseen by the staff of the L. H. Bailey Hortorium at Cornell University. Very expensive but worth talking your local library into acquiring if they haven't already.

Huxley, Anthony, ed. *Garden Perennials and Water Plants.* New York: Macmillan, 1971.
A fine pocket guide with colorful illustrations. Some juggling of information is necessary as the book is entirely English, but still worthwhile.

————*Mountain Flowers.* New York: Macmillan, 1972.
Attractively illustrated and thorough guide to alpine flowers.

Jekyll, Gertrude. *Annuals and Biennials.* London: Country Life, n.d.
The classic English gardener talks about the classic English approach to these flowers. Just as good today as ever. Look for the reprints by the Antique Collectors' Club.

————*Colour Schemes for the Flower Garden.* London: Country Life, 1936.
Another gem by Miss Jekyll. Both the photos and advice are as up-to-date as the day they were written.

Johnson, Hugh. *The Principles of Gardening.* New York: Simon & Schuster, 1979.
A classic guide to the practice of gardening, covering art, history, and science with fine illustrations, good advice, and readable text. Should be in every serious library.

Lancaster, Roy. *Trees for Your Garden.* New York: Scribner's, 1974.
Trees from very small to very large, all described and recommended for the garden.

Lees-Milne, Alvilde, and Rosemary Verey. *The Englishwoman's Garden.* London: Chatto & Windus, 1980.
Gardens designed and worked by amateurs. A beautiful book full of fine gardens and ideas. There is a new volume in the works devoted to the Englishman's garden. This is another book that belongs in any basic garden library.

Lloyd, Christopher. *Foliage Plants.* London: Collins, 1973.
A literate discussion of plants to grow for leaves instead of flowers. Though English, the philosophy fits anywhere.

———*The Well-Tempered Garden.* New York: Dutton, 1970.
An absolutely wonderful book to read—and own. Should be consulted every year before picking up a shovel.

Lloyd, Francis Ernest. *The Carnivorous Plants.* New York: Dover, 1976.
Another good Dover reprint of a book that covers all you ever would want to know about carnivorous plants.

Miles, Bebe. *Wildflower Perennials for Your Garden.* New York: Hawthorne, 1976.
The classic American book on wildflowers for the garden. Covers everything from basic design to completion. A must!

Pizzetti, Ippolito, and Henry Cocker. *Flowers: A Guide for Your Garden.* 2 vols. New York: Harry N. Abrams, 1975.
Using the fine color plates from the great eighteenth- and nineteenth-century botanical periodicals for a starting-off point, these books cover both history and culture of a host of garden annuals and perennials. Books for consulting when winter winds blow.

Reader's Digest Encyclopedia of Garden Plants and Flowers. London: The Reader's Digest Association Limited, 1971.
Though a British encyclopedia, most of the information is easily translated to an American garden. Thorough and well done. Either invest in it or get the library to do the same.

Schacht, Wilhelm. *Rock Gardens.* New York: Universe, 1981.
An updated classic on rock gardens and a fine book to own.

Seike, Kiyoshi; Masanobu Kudō, and David H. Engel. *A Japanese Touch for Your Garden.* New York: Kodansha, 1980.
A great introduction to the beauties of gardening in the Japanese style, with endless ideas and clear instructions on planning. Good to have in the library.

Thompson, Mildred L., and Edward J. Thompson. *Begonias: The Complete Reference Guide.* New York: Times Books, 1981.
The most complete—and visually interesting—guide to the study and care of begonias available today. For those who specialize in these plants, this is a must-have book.

Welch, Humphrey J. *Manual of Dwarf Conifers.* New York: Theophrastus/Garland, 1979.
A complete listing of all the dwarf conifers in existence today,

with photos of specimens in the garden or landscape. A good reference.

Wolgensinger, Bernard, and José Daidone. *The Personal Garden: Its Architecture and Design.* New York: Van Nostrand Reinhold, 1975.

An absolutely wonderful picture book that makes the reader want to never stop making gardens.

Wyman, Donald. *Wyman's Gardening Encyclopedia.* New York: Macmillan, 1971.

The one-volume American garden book. Another must for the garden library.

Index

Illustrations are listed in boldface